A WOMAN LOVES UNTIL A MAN LIES

A WOMAN LOVES UNTIL A MAN LIES

THE DATING CYCLE

TAMARA ARMOUR

TATE PUBLISHING
AND ENTERPRISES, LLC

Published by Tate Publishing & Enterprises, LLC
127 E. Trade Center Terrace | Mustang, Oklahoma 73064 USA
1.888.361.9473 | www.tatepublishing.com

Tate Publishing is committed to excellence in the publishing industry. The company reflects the philosophy established by the founders, based on Psalm 68:11,
"The Lord gave the word and great was the company of those who published it."

Published in the United States of America

ISBN: 978-1-62994-289-6
1. Family & Relationships / Love & Romance
2. Self-Help / General
13.11.22

DEDICATION

Dedicated to God, my family (for their love and support), and all the women.

CONTENTS

INTRODUCTION

I wrote this book for all women. What I really wanted to do was expose the truth about maintaining a healthy and successful relationship. Today, many women are convinced that it is just something about them that repels men.

Dozens of women have fallen into the trap of being led into a cat-and-mouse game that does not lead anywhere but to a broken and confused heart. In this book, I hope to give women a clearer picture of catching the right man, maintaining a successful stress-free relationship, and finding happiness in yourself that no man can take away.

MR. RIGHT: HAS THIS MAN BECOME EXTINCT?

As a woman, I can tell you that there are a lot of women out there that would actually like to meet a good man but believe they are extinct in today's society. A woman wants a man that is going to love and care for her. He will be faithful to just one woman. He must have a job and must not ask a woman for money to take care of him. It would be fair to say that most women are looking for this kind of man, but it seems like he does not exist. Has he become extinct or is he still out there?

The good man is still out there in the world. He is real and he does exist. The only problem is: he is compared to many men that have done so many women wrong. He is the man who will open a door for you. He is the man that will take time to get to know you. He will not constantly pressure you for sex because he will care about you. He will not ask you for money and will not ask you to do all of the work in the relationship. If he had to pick between you or Halle Berry, he would pick you! When you meet someone that is truly right for you and is interested in you, then you're going to be on his brain.

A lot of women have met men that were not right for them, but they still tried to make it work. A good man will not be a perfect man but he will be perfect for you. If you are not willing to accept him for who he is then look for a man with the characteristics of what you are looking for. With that being said, it is important to be realistic in your approach of finding a man. Do not look to mold a man into the type of man that you would like for him to be based on your experiences and perspectives. Allow him to be himself but look for qualities in a man that tell you if he is a good man in the way that he treats you. The main question that you need to ask yourself is: "How does this man treat me?" Does he talk to me like he does not respect me, or does he think that I am dumb? Does he call me, or do I do all of the calling? Does he want to take me out on dates, or does he just want to sit at the house and never do anything in public with me? Does he get irritated with me a lot? Is he willing to be faithful? Does he answer your calls when you call or does it seem like he does not make an effort to talk to you and you are doing all of the calling and all of the work in the relationship.

What happens to a lot of women is they begin to settle. They no longer believe that the good man exists, so they start to compromise. They begin looking for the man with the least amount of issues. While they know that they need to wait to be with someone else, loneliness sets in so they choose a man that is tolerable in a least favorable situation. For example: a woman has three men. The first man has a decent job and a running car, but he cheats a lot. He does pay for a couple of meals, but he barely calls or spends time with her. The second man does not have a job, but he does have a car and does not cheat. He doesn't pay for any meals, but as long as she is paying, then he spends as much time with her as she wants. The third man does not have a car or a job, and a dog has more morals when it comes to sex than he does. He actually calls her too much. It gets to the point where she actually hates to pick up the phone, as he always calls her either for money or for sex. Which man does she choose? Which one is the tolerable choice out of a least favorable situation? She's lonely and she wants to be with a man, none exists, so she feels that she might as well settle for the one that has the least issues.

That is where the problem starts. She gets hurt and that's when the right man comes along. She has so many issues that he says he cannot deal with it. He wasn't there when the woman was getting treated poorly, so why should he be blamed for what some other man was responsible for? There are so many men that have so many issues nowadays that they make all men look bad. Some men try to play like they are good men when they are really not. They do not pay for meals. They only want sex and money from a woman and they cheat on various women. That is not a good man by any means.

However, what makes a woman different from other women is not her looks but her personality. If it was just about looks and body shape, then what would be the deciding factor in him choosing you over another woman? There would always be someone with a prettier face or a better-looking body. Looks may be able to catch a man, but personality is what keeps him. A real man will see the natural beauty in you that connects with his heart and soul. He's not going to tear you down, but instead he will uplift you.

Does this man sound too good to be true? No, he isn't. In today's world, it seems like most men no longer practice chivalry. However, although most of them have abandoned this system, chivalry is not dead. When a guy really cares about you, he is not going to treat you badly. Think about it this way: how do you treat the things in your life that you really care about?

You tend to carelessly handle those things that you don't really care much about. On the other hand, the things we really do care about, we take care of. Think of your favorite pair of blue jeans. It doesn't matter if these jeans have holes or faded spots because they have a special place in your heart. People may even tell you to get rid of them and buy a new pair, but you know you could never part with them. Well that's how a man feels about someone he cares about. He doesn't care what anyone else says; he keeping you. You're just that special. No matter how many jeans walk by him, he's never trading in that special pair of jeans.

So where is this special man? You may have tried to look for him while attending church, logging on to dating sites, working out at the gym, shopping at the mall, playing games at the arcade, visiting the local library, strolling in the park, walking down the street, going on blind dates, and maybe even dancing at a club.

But over and over, you're disappointed and meet the opposite of what you're looking for. Where is he then?

He is out there in the world. There are still many good men out there in the world today, but they are spread out so that there is hope in the world. Keep your heart and your eyes open so you are able to see this man when he happens to walk into your life. Trying to find him in different places like the library, church, and coffee shops does not work. Although there is a good chance that you would meet the right man in these places, it is not enough to simply go out to these places and expect to meet him on a particular day and place.

If that were the case, then we'll be all out doing it. A good man will not be in places where there are drugs and violence. He keeps himself out of trouble by living a simple but fun life. He doesn't have to be knocked out drunk and high to have a good time. I'm not saying a good man will not drink. But he will not put himself in a wrong situation. There's nothing wrong with seeing someone at a party or even going to a bar and ordering drinks. But do not look for a good man that hangs out every weekend at clubs and parties. This tells you that he flirts a lot and may not be looking for a serious commitment right now. So watch the places that you talk to men because that will tell you a lot about their character and what they are into.

For instance, a man that hangs out a lot at a bookstore likes to read and may enjoy discussing different points about books or ideas. A man that often works out at the gym or plays sports is into being active and athletic. A man that attends church activities often enjoys being social and volunteering his time for the benefit of others. A man that enjoys swimming and going to the beach may be romantic and likes the feel of nature and getting close to it. Be very careful where you look for or talk to guys. The atmosphere and surroundings tell you a lot about his personality and character.

What I am about to say will be shocking and maybe even upsetting, but it is the truth. There is no guaranteed way to find a man. You have to be patient and wait for the right one to come along. How many times have we become impatient and decided to pick up anything because we were lonely? Everyone has a specific time that they are supposed to meet that special one. You can't plan it. You don't know when it will be. Although you may not be able to plan when you will meet the man of your dreams, you can keep your heart safe so that you can receive him when you do meet him. You'll be surprised by how many women have been through so much with men that they actually turn a good man away when they do meet them. It's not that they do not want a good man. They have probably been looking for them their whole life. It's just that they have met some men that were no good and when the right man did arrive, their hearts were scared and wounded. They just couldn't take another scratch. Although you may not be able to predict when and where you may meet, one thing you can do is protect your heart from the wrong men so that you will be able to meet a good man when the time presents itself.

Have you ever been in a bad relationship that made you hesitate to speak to men again? You don't care if he was a so-called "good" man or the most "rotten" man on the face on the earth. When our hearts get robbed by the wrong men, they take love away from the right man. So we get hurt, and then every man becomes the same. We might not realize it, but the right man could have walked into our life but we were too hurt to see him.

One common thing that women do when they are hurt is that they put up a guard so no one can get in. That means no man can get in, not even the good ones. Or women tend to put up a flag that says, "Anybody, please rescue me!"—which pretty much lets anyone in who they feel can heal the pain. Some men take advantage of this flag and use women while their self-esteem is low. Of course, every woman is different. One woman will experience pain in a different way than another. There are those who block their heart from all men after being hurt, and there are others who give a free pass to any man they think can heal the pain.

It is not your fault. No one walks into a relationship saying, "This person is going to hurt me and I just can't wait." With that said, it is important to remember that life is a learning experience. As Henry Ford said, "A mistake is a chance to begin again more intelligently." The worst thing that you can do after being involved in a bad relationship is to get into another one. It's kind of like having a drinking problem and going into a bar. We all know that is not going to work. Getting into another relationship after being hurt is the same thing. Getting into a relationship too quickly after your previous relationship can lower a woman's self esteem.

One thing that it does is it makes your standards go down. I'm not talking about the kind of standards that are cocky and unreachable. I'm talking about the standards that say you have value and you do not deserve every low scum that walk the earth. This is a cry that says, "Anyone, rescue me." On the other hand, when some women get hurt, their standards become unrealistic and unreachable. They believe that no one is good enough to be with them. Therefore their standards become so high that subconsciously they believe that this will prevent any man from ever hurting them again. So they look for the "perfect" unobtainable man that will never hurt them. Let's look at Karen's relationship.

WHO'S THERE? ON GUARD!

Karen was the typical 23-year-old who had not been in many relationships. She met her first true love, John, at 21. Things were good for the first two months or so. Then she began to notice that John was not all that into her like he used to be. He stopped calling her every day like he used to. If she called him, John would not return her calls until four or five hours afterwards. What was so strange was that he used to return her calls in fifteen minutes or less. Sometimes he would even call her right back before she had a chance to put down the phone. Now, when they talked on the phone, there was a lot of silence and it seemed as if he couldn't wait to hang up. He really didn't want her to touch him, and he always pointed out everything that he thought was wrong with her. He was always comparing her to other women. John would also flirt constantly with other women right in front of her. Karen began to believe that he did not care for her at all.

But she remembered how he was in the beginning of their relationship. He was so sweet and caring. He was always there for her. He picked her up from her job and called her throughout the day. She began to notice that he only called her at certain times. He called her late at night and very early in the morning. Karen became confused. What did she do to make him stop acting like he did at first? So Karen tried harder to make the relationship work. She thought up little cute ways to tell John that she loved him. She made an effort to get off of work early to spend time with him when she could. She took little short breaks to call him and left little sweet messages on his voice mail. She even bought him little gifts just to let him know that she was just thinking about him. Surely, after John saw she was taking the initiative to save her relationship then he would start doing the same too. This went on for about three months before Karen realized that the romantic things she was doing were only pushing John away. He accepted the gifts, but he always wanted something more. They spent time together, but it always ended in an argument. The sweet messages became irritating because Karen talked to John's voice mail more than to him.

Karen began to notice that John's phone would ring a lot but he never answered the phone. When he did answer, he always had to leave the room. Immediately after he returned, he always had somewhere that he had to go with his friends. Karen didn't want to seem like she was nagging him, so she tried her best to act like everything was fine. She thought that he was seeing another woman, but she was going to fight for her man. Karen felt that their relationship needed to go to the next level. She read a relationship book that said that men liked a challenge, but if you waited too long, they became discouraged. Karen was proud that she made John wait five months before they had sex. But she felt that she might have made him wait too long and he was becoming discouraged. Karen planned the perfect evening. She decided to invite John over. She cooked the perfect meal and she put on her favorite dress. She lit candles and threw rose petals all over her room. John was late. Their date was at 7:00 p.m. It was going on 8:45 p.m. She called John three times before he answered. John said that he had some things that came up and he would not be able to see her until after 10:00 p.m. At this point Karen was fed up. She felt like she was the only one in the relationship, and she was doing all the work. She wanted this relationship to work but it was a lot of work. It seemed like she was giving and giving and John was not giving anything back. Karen really wanted to see him. She wanted to make John like her so she bit her tongue and agreed to 10:00 p.m. John promised her that he would be there at 10:00 p.m. Karen decided to flip on the TV to pass some of the time. Karen kept looking at the clock. It was going on 10:20 and John still had not shown up. She called him again but got his voice mail. She left six messages for him to call her back before he finally showed up unannounced at her door around 11:40.

Karen's eyes were red from crying. And she was in no mood to see John anymore. She was angry and upset. She had spent a lot of time planning the evening to save their relationship and John did not even care. He did apologize for being late but he told Karen that he was over at his mom's house and he lost track of time. John saw the candles and rose petals on the floor. So he promised Karen that he would try to save their relationship by being a better boyfriend. He did tell Karen that he felt like she did not really want to be with him because she waited so long to be intimate in their relationship.

Karen knew that she probably should not become intimate with John after all that he put her through, but she thought this final act of her love for him would bring them closer. After that night, things became worse between them. John no longer wanted anything to do with Karen. The last four months of their relationship consisted of arguments. They would break up every two weeks and then get back together. Finally John decided to cut off the relationship and Karen was heartbroken.

Karen immediately dated a guy a month after the breakup with John. This guy was nothing like John, but Karen constantly compared him to her ex. There was nothing that this new guy could do to make up for her ex's past mistakes. Evan was a pretty good guy that had just got out of a two-year relationship. He was really looking for someone that wanted to be in a committed relationship. He wanted to take things slow, but he definitely wanted to be with someone who also wanted a stable relationship. But it did not matter what Evan said or did, as Karen would always make him seem like a bad guy. If he was five minutes late for their date, she would get upset and cancel the whole date. If he bought her a gift, she would get upset and tell him to take it back. Every time they talked on the phone, she did not really feel like talking. Evan became very discouraged after a while and decided to just be friends with Karen. This time, she was going to break it off with the guy before he broke it off with her. She was not too surprised. She knew that this was coming. After the relationship was over, Karen wrote Evan a long letter explaining her last relationship. She told him that she knew he was going to leave because all men are the same.

Karen was not a bad person. She was just a hurt person who decided to get into another relationship before she had healed from her first one. Looking back on her relationship with John,

Karen was the one doing all the work in the relationship. John was not taking any initiative to do the same. Karen kept giving in the relationship while John was not making any effort at all. But if a guy is really interested in you, he will usually make the first move. He initiates dates. He calls you. He leaves you sweet messages and buys you thoughtful gifts. If a man is really into you, you won't have to worry about why he hasn't called you. You won't have to worry about him not wanting to spend time with you because he will want to spend time with you. Of course, he will have a life and want to do some other things, but you will never have to worry about him trying to schedule you in. He will definitely fit you into his schedule because he actually wants to be with you.

BEING THE PERSON YOU WANT TO ATTRACT

There is nothing wrong with having standards and wanting someone that will treat you right. But do not have double standards or be hypocritical with your standards. I have heard some women say, "I know I'm big, but I can't be with a big guy." You can't put eyes on love; do not say that you cannot date a guy with a few extra pounds when you have a few extra pounds. We all have preferences and there is nothing wrong with having them. But you also have to be the kind of person that you want to attract. I've also heard some women say that they cannot date a man that does not have himself together yet they do not have a job or a car. When you become hypercritical in your approach to finding a man, then that only causes problems in the relationship later. There is nothing wrong with having standards but do not be unrealistic in having very high expectations of him but not of yourself.

If you do not want a man that lies to you then do not lie to him or anyone for that matter. If you do not want a man that cheats on you then do not be a cheater. If you want a man that cares for you then be the kind of person that cares about other people. There are some women out in the world today that want to catch a good man, but they have let their values and morals decay. So, always be the kind of person that you want to attract. Although there are a lot of people in the world today that use and mistreat other people, don't become like them. Stay true to yourself and always treat people with the same respect that you would want them to have for you.

PERSONAL HYGIENE

Always look for personal hygiene in a man. If he goes out on dates with you and he is dirty or his clothes have holes and stains, then leave him alone. He is very careless and does not care about himself and his hygiene. He certainly does not have a get-up-and-go attitude and will not be selective in the people he sleeps with. If he wears baggy clothes, then he is into image and how his peers view him than having his own identity. I'm not saying his clothes should be skintight, but if this guy wears his pants off his butt, there's a chance that he cares more about impressing others than being who he really is. So always look at how a man dresses because it tells a lot about his character as well as his goals and ambitions in life. That does not say that he has to be wearing a tuxedo or anything to have goals. Hygiene means that he cares about himself and how he looks.

LET'S TRADE

Another thing that most relationship books do not expose is the fact that you cannot determine the right time to be intimate with a man. Every woman is different and has different beliefs. I am in no way telling you to sleep with a man on the first date just because he may like you. What I am saying is never become intimate with a man if you are not ready. If a guy truly cares about you, then he will wait on you. Otherwise, he will leave if you decide to wait to become intimate with him. Having sex with him will not make him stay if that is not his choice to do so. What makes a man stay in a relationship is that he chooses to stay. A woman can wait five years before becoming intimate with a man but that will not make him care for her. If a man doesn't care for you, waiting ten years will not change his mind. A man has to make a choice to care about you. Becoming intimate or withholding sex will not influence the decision that he has made. The only thing that does is to put more stress and heartbreak on you because you wonder why your techniques did not work.

Sex should be something that is done with someone that you love. Sometimes a woman will trade sex in order to get love from a man. She really does not want to have sex, but she feels that if she has sex, then eventually he will grow to love her. Some men will prove this theory wrong. They can be in a relationship for seven years and not grow to love the woman at all. So be very careful when asking for exchanges because there is no guarantee that you will not get ripped off. You may do it only to find out that the exchange on his end comes up short or there is no love involved at all. So before deciding to have sex with a man, make sure that you're not trying to exchange anything, because more often than not, this exchange will leave you with a hole in your bag and some lost merchandise.

Having sex with the wrong person can make you stay in bad relationships longer because of the bond that sex creates. If sex is done with the wrong man, then after he gets that from you, he would have no reason to call you until he needs it again. Most men will always keep the communication lines open for the next time that they want to do it again. But the amount of time that he gives you will be limited and will always be on his terms. Before spending time with you again, he will always have to think about what's in it for him. Also, once he has had sex with you, then he knows that there will be some emotional attachment there, so he makes sure that he keeps his distance for a while so that you do not become clingy.

Some men, after they have had sex with you, will not call you back. They feel that they have conquered the territory that they set out to get, and now it is time to move on to another one. This type of man will leave whether you give him sex or not. His main intention was not to get to know you at all, so he only gives you a certain time to have sex. If he does not get it within that time frame, he moves on. If he does, he still moves on. You may get a call or two afterwards but that is it. To him, he got what he came for so he moves on.

It is easy to understand why most women feel like men leave after sex. They associate the relationship going fine before they had sex. Then once they had sex, the guy left. So there are many women out there that feel like if you have sex with a man, then he will leave; and if you don't, then he will stay. That is not true at all. With that said, do not have sex with a man until you are ready no matter how much he asks for it. In the long run, it affects the woman if the relationship does not work because she feels it's her fault for not having sex too soon or not waiting long enough. And women feel like they have to create all kinds of formulas to help them determine the ideal number of times that they should withhold sex from men before he gets discouraged and leaves. But there is no magic number. If he stayed, it was not anything the woman did that worked. He chose to for whatever reason that was in his mind at that time. It was an individual choice on his part.

Some women on the other hand may have had better experiences associated with sex. They may actually feel that having sex early in a relationship makes the man stay versus withholding it from him. They may feel that he is going to get it somewhere else if they do not take care of him, so why make him wait and risk losing him? That is also not true. He stayed because he wanted to. He made a conscious choice to stay. Sex might have been a factor on his mind at the time, but it definitely was not the prevailing reason that made him stay.

So make sure that when you do have sex, it is your choice and is not influenced by a feeling that he will leave if you do not have sex and he will stay if you do. I can promise you that if he stays or leaves, then he had that intent from the beginning of the relationship before you both were intimate. When a man first meets you, he knows what he wants from you. He decides if he just wants to talk or if he wants sex or money from you. Sometimes his intent may change after he talks to you, and he may debate over what he wants from you, but never think sex influenced a man's decision to stay.

Remember be sure this is what you want to do. If you are not ready for anything to happen, then never go to a guy's house to or let him come to yours. There are still men out there that know what the word "no" means. There are also some men out there that will argue that if you weren't looking for anything to happen, then you would not have been there. So remember: if you are not ready, then meet in public places for dates. Never go back to a man's place or invite him into yours if you're not ready to go to the next level. Do not send mixed signals. Do not tease and flirt about it, and then say that you are not ready. Most men will not take this to be flirting. Once you have sex with a man, it's hard for him to accept later on that you want to wait to have sex with him again. In his mind, he is thinking, if you're not ready, then why have sex? He has already gotten used to going further with you and he does not want to wait. Instead, he will view it like you're playing games with him. So until you are ready, do not indicate for more if that is not how you are feeling.

Things change once you do have sex with a man. The first thing a man will tell you is it will not. But it actually does. Just because you give a man sex does not necessarily mean that he will leave. But the whole dynamics of the relationship will. For instance, if you were so used to being truthful and honest with a man before you had sex, then after you have sex, he will hold back his bluntness and start to keep some things inside rather than express them like he might have did before. The reason for this is because he was motivated to do that to keep having sex with you. So in his mind, he feels like he cannot say certain things that he had said before and continue to keep having sex with you. So I'm not saying that he will lie to you, but he will be very careful of what he says to you because he knows that you will get upset and withhold sex from him. So he does not want to do anything to mess up continuing to be intimate with you.

Take love slowly and remember that sex should be something special between two people. You're worth waiting for if that is what you chose to do. Many women lose their virginity because they feel like if they do not give the guy what he wants, then other women will. This messes the woman up because she starts to feel ashamed and guilty if the guy leaves because she gave up her virginity to a guy that cared nothing about her in the end. Whether you are a virgin or not, I want to encourage you to always make the decision for yourself and not do anything because you feel the guy wants you to.

Karen should have waited before she got into another relationship. Everybody's healing time is different. Some women need two years. Some women may only need four or five months to heal after a bad relationship. When it is time to move on, make sure that you have forgiven your ex. Only judge the new guy in your life for the things that he does. Karen could not fully open up to Evan because she was not over her last relationship with John. The worst thing you can do to a sore is to peel off the scab before it has healed. Evan could have been a great guy for Karen. Because she was hurt, she put her guard up and would not let Evan in. It is okay to take the relationship slow before you give your heart to a guy. What Karen did was she closed her heart to all men. Without taking the sufficient time to really heal from her last relationship, she began to reenact her last relationship in her current one. She could not separate what John did from Evan. No one was going to hurt her again, so she built up a wall to her heart. You can't knock down brick. This technique keeps everyone out. Evan did not understand that Karen was still hurting from her last relationship. All he understood was Karen was treating him unfairly for something that he did not do to her.

"HELP ME, I'M DROWNING! ANYONE, PLEASE?"

The "rescue me, anyone" mentality is not that uncommon among hurting women. In fact, this mentality is becoming a common practice in today's dating society. Many women's self-esteem is affected each year because they are accepting any man into their lives. There can be many factors as to why women experience low self-esteem. Many women have been teased by men while they have been growing up (emotionally abused) which caused them to develop low self-esteem. Some women have been sexually or physically abused which psychologically devastated them and led them to believe that something was wrong with them or that they caused the abuse. Other issues with self-esteem might stem from always being compared to other siblings who were thought to be the ideal of success in the family. Many women might have developed self-esteem issues when they began to get into relationships with men. Some of these men compared them to other women and made them feel they were not smart or pretty enough. This made the women feel inferior and ashamed to be themselves. A lot of women develop low self-esteem just by looking at magazines or comparing themselves to many standards of beauty in the media, not realizing that many of the pictures are airbrushed or that many of these women may have undergone plastic surgery.

KEEP LOOKING AT HER!

Women are constantly given an image to compare themselves to in the media. It seems like the media is consistently and creatively finding new ways to say, "Hey, look at her. Don't you wish you were her? Look how pretty she is. Look at all the men that she gets. Be like her and you could have her life too." The woman being portrayed always has long hair. They appear to have the perfect skin and the perfect shape, while always having perfect breasts and a bottom to match. Women are receiving too many mixed messages from the media that confuse them into believing that they have to be anybody but themselves.

It's important to understand that looks are not as important like society would have you believe. It might even argue that you can get up the work chain without hard work if you are pretty. Or that many men will buy you things and want to date you. Maybe you may feel that being rejected so much in your life is caused by your looks or lack of looks. If it was so true that a man would not cheat on you if you were pretty, then why is it that some of the most beautiful women in the world deal with relationship problems and cheating issues just like any other woman in America?

Looks can only go so far. Many men are captivated by a woman's looks, but she has to have something beyond looks to keep him. Men get bored very easily. So there must not only be physical attraction between men and women, but a deeper connection as well. That is one of the reasons that may cause many men to cheat on women although the women may be considered to be very attractive.

You will never be able to be anybody but you. The low self-esteem comes from trying to be what everybody wants you to be or looking for a man to tell you who you are. Let me tell you about what happened to Tracy:

Tracy was 26, and she was pretty and smart. She was the average woman looking for a man to sweep her off her feet and carry her off into a fairy-tale romance. Tracy had been teased a lot while she was growing up, so she always thought of herself as someone that wasn't very pretty. She wanted to be any other woman other than herself. Most men would say that Tracy was naturally pretty and attractive. Tracy did not feel like she was pretty because she always compared herself to other women and what men said about her. Tracy did not have a positive image of herself. From the time she learned how to read, she would compare herself to models in the magazines. She would study the pictures over and over, and then go look in the mirror to compare her image to theirs. Tracy knew that she should like herself for who she was, but she needed those pictures to tell her if she was pretty or not.

Becoming sexually active at the age of sixteen, Tracy would sometimes become intimate with men just to feel loved and attractive. Tracy was never without a boyfriend. She always needed a man to define who she was. If she did not have a man around, then she felt she did not have an identity. Some of the men that she dated were okay, but some of them were really mean to her. They constantly cheated on her or told her things to lower her self-esteem. They compared her to other women and acted like they did not want to be bothered with her. Tracy began to accept any man into her life because she did not know her value. By the age of twenty-six, Tracy had been with many men that had physically and mentally abused her.

She no longer believed that her life meant anything without a man. Ultimately, the last relationship Tracy was in sent her to the emergency room. Tracy suffered six cracked ribs, two black eyes, and a broken nose. Tracy was released from the hospital only to return to the abusive relationship. Tracy did go back to the hospital, but this time she was sent to the intensive care unit. Tracy stayed in that relationship four years before she finally left.

Two months later, Tracy met a man that took nude pictures of her and posted it on the Internet. He also sold her pictures and introduced her to a few amateur porn companies. Three years later, Tracy died of AIDS.

What makes Tracy's story so sad is the fact that many women are in relationships with men because they feel like they are defined by a man. True, many women in the early 1900s were only noticed in society by their husband. It was not proper for a woman to be alone or single past a certain age. Women were in fact not even allowed to divorce a man that was abusive to them. Divorce was frowned upon by society at the time. Being socially correct meant that women did not divorce their husbands without proper cause. Women at one time could not vote, own property in their name, bear witness in court, serve on a jury, attend major universities, and the list continues. Now, women are defined for more than being in the shadow of a man. There is certainly nothing wrong with having a man. It only becomes wrong when women lose their life and their identity for it.

Many women today might not be in a severe situation as Tracy but even emotional abuse is just as harmful. Each word tears apart a woman's self-esteem until there is nothing left. The good news is low self-esteem can be cured. It will not be an easy process, but in the end it is life-saving. In order to get to the root of low-self esteem, it is better to figure out when it first started and who it started with. Low self-esteem cannot be covered with a bandage. The wound must be opened up so that it can become visible. Once the wound is identified, then it can be treated with the right medicine and healing can be applied. When you get up in the morning and look in the mirror, say that you are the most beautiful person in the world. You don't have to attribute this factor to your looks only. Believe you are beautiful just for being you, no matter what you may look like. You may not like your hair or your nose but you are beautiful. What you think may be a flaw may be your best feature in the eyes of another person. The only cure to low self-esteem is to begin to like yourself for who you are. If you're not happy with yourself then men will be able to tell. And how can you expect someone else to appreciate you if you don't even like yourself?

"I CAN BE NO ONE BUT ME"

How long should a woman wait before she gets in her next relationship? That is a question that only you can answer. You should not move into another relationship until you have forgiven the other person for what they did to you. And the most important person you should forgive is yourself. A lot of times women look back and blame themselves for the relationship not working out. They go down the list and point out everything that they think is wrong with them. *It was my hair. I'm too fat. I'm not thick enough. I'm not smart enough. I wasn't pretty enough.* They start with their appearance and then move on to the inside. *I'm so boring. I'm stupid. I'm too shy. I can't do anything right. I'm not good enough to be with him.* Finally, they start comparing themselves to other women. Eventually they start changing into the kind of woman that they think men want to be with. One reason for the sudden change is that they are afraid to be themselves. They were rejected before in previous relationships, so now they believe they can never be their true self to make a man like them.

It's okay to look back at a relationship for a little while to see some of the things that you could have done differently. The only reason for looking back is so that we do not make the same mistakes again. If you're dwelling on the past, it will not change it. The only thing the past does is keep you from receiving something new because the past can only give you something old. In order to have a new relationship with new experiences, you have to throw away those old negative memories. Learn from them and then throw them away.

Sometimes when we talk to people with so much wisdom, it may seem that they were just born with it. But what you may not realize is experience plays a very important key. They have wisdom on a lot of things because they learned from their mistakes. They made some mistakes but they did not keep making them. So if a similar situation ever arose again, they were able to recall their experiences from the past and that stopped them from making the same mistake again.

So I encourage you not to look at your mistakes as something that can hold you back but rather as experiences that push you forward to not make the same mistakes again. Everybody has fallen at one time but it's the winners that are not afraid to get back up.

"I DON'T MIND WORKING; I JUST DON'T WANT TO BE THE ONLY ONE!"

Trying to do too much in a relationship without any work from the other person leaves you stressed out and tired. When you see that the man in the relationship is not doing his part, that's when you have to back up and re-evaluate the relationship. Don't keep giving and giving until you finally have given your all. Let the man give to the relationship too. Once you see he wants to spend time with you then by all means give a little. Once you see that he is making an effort to call you, return his calls. I am a firm believer that you cannot buy a person's affection. If they do not accept you without the gift-giving then they are not going to accept you. You shouldn't have to buy someone's affection. It should be given freely. If you are in a relationship with a man that constantly asks for your money: run. He is just trying to use you as an ATM machine. Any man worth having will have something to offer you. Not just in terms of money but in terms of time, conversations, and appreciating who you are.

Don't ever make excuses for a man. If you're the only one doing all the calling, then he is not that into you. Men are different from women in the way they think and react to certain situations. I hear women say this all the time. "I thought we connected but it's been almost a week and he has not returned my phone calls. Men are so confusing."

The first thought that comes to mind is maybe he did not get the calls or he was busy. No, that is not it. If he were busy at the time, then he would make sure that he called you back later that day and explained why. He might not have gone into great detail but if he really wanted to talk to you, he would either answer the phone and tell you that he would call you back or he would call you back later when he had some free time. If you do all of the calling and he only answers back to your calls or texts days later, then he is saying that he is not into you like you are into him.

Although men do not come right out and say that they do not like you or really wish you would stop calling, they do throw out hints. They tell you through their actions rather than their words. If a man disrespects you through his actions then it's the same as if he actually said, "I really don't care for you."

Both his words and his actions should line up. You do have some men that are very suave with their words with the ladies. If you're not careful, you can fall into his trap just by how smooth his words are. He can say that he wants to spend time with you and he cares about you, but his actions are saying that he does not care for you at all. So don't make excuses for men. If a guy tells you that he likes spending time with you but never calls and never wants to take you out on dates, then you don't have to call up ten girlfriends to analyze the situation. He just does not care about you.

Many women need to hear a man say that he is not into her before it can actually hit home that this guy decided that he did not want to pursue anything with her. That is discouraging because most guys don't really come out and tell women. But whether you hear his words or not, learn to look for these signs that let you know that he may not be into you:

1. He does not call you. When he does return your calls, it is days later. Most of the time he may be feeling bored or kind of guilty. So he decides to call with an excuse as to why he couldn't call you back. Usually, this is done so you can stop calling as much. For instance, he may say that he was out of town or he was sick. If the excuse seems too farfetched to you, then nine times out of ten, he is lying.

2. You can only text him. He never calls you, and when you call him, he responds back with a text. A lot of times, men will have extra friends outside of their relationship. Basically, this means he has someone (whether he has a girlfriend or he is married), there is certainly nothing wrong with texting. But if you text him, and you both never talk on the phone then something is wrong. You both may actually prefer to text, but if you can only text him and you can never talk to him on the phone then be cautious. With the advancements in technology today, a man can text another woman and be watching a movie with his girlfriend. All he has to do is put his phone on vibrate or silent. His girlfriend or wife does not suspect a thing because he could be checking his e-mail or just texting one of his boys back.

3. If he does call you, it's late at night, early in the morning, or right after he gets off work. Most men that are in relationships wait until their woman goes to work before they call. It's always a pattern with this guy. You can plan his calls like clockwork. If you call him outside of his schedule, then you can always expect to get his voicemail. And he calls you back on schedule. There may be a weekend that he detours from his schedule because his girl or wife is out of town or hanging out with her friends and will be gone for a while. But basically you can never get in touch with this man except for certain times.

4. He never takes you out. You both meet at his place or he comes to yours. If a man never wants to take you out in the beginning of the relationship, then he already has someone. He is just hoping to have you on the side and have fun with you without ever committing. Some men want to test the waters and have a relationship outside of what they already have. Not all men are like this. But there are a good majority of men that feel that this is okay.

5. He pressures you for sex way too early in the dating process. He pressures you the first day that you both meet. He wants sex from you and it hasn't even been a week. If he is telling you that he wants to have a relationship with you but he wants sex too early in the relationship, then he only wants sex from you. But he feels that you will not give it to him unless he decodes his words and have you believe that he wants more. If a man is going to stay, he is going to stay but real men will not expect sex on the first date.

6. When he talks to you on the phone, he always sounds depressed to talk to you and you talk no longer than five minutes. He always promises to call you back, only to end up doing so five days later. The flip side to that is that he calls you too much. He calls you like ten times a day to talk off and on. Just because a guy calls you a lot does not mean that he wants to be with you and has good intentions. Some men believe women like to talk on the phone so he overdoes the gesture. He wants to try to make you believe that he is really into you because he calls you all the time. He knows how women complain about never being able to reach some men so he overdoes the phone calls. A lot of times this type of man is seeing different women so he might also call a lot to make sure that you are not on your way to see him while he is with another woman. So he

may really be calling to find out your location rather than calling to actually hear from you.

7. This man plays mind games with you. Some men will actually push you to the limit to see how far he can go with you. He will test your emotional stability to learn your weaknesses and how he can use them to manipulate you. How does he do it? Simple. He talks to you and makes you feel comfortable opening up about your life. To you, you are just answering simple questions and sharing information. He has told you a lot of stuff so you feel comfortable opening up and telling him stuff. Then, when he is comfortable that he has learned you and your behavior, he starts to let a little of the real him come out slowly. He has already calculated that there may be some surprises along the way, but ultimately he feels that he knows you well enough to begin playing games. He may even start to make hurtful and nasty comments. He was so sweet before so this takes you off guard. The reason why he feels that he can do this is that he feels like you are not going to do or say anything to him. I'm not telling you to guard your behavior. Never do that. Be you but when a man starts playing games with you, never be afraid to stand up for yourself and let him know that you demand respect. You do not have to cuss him out to do it. You can be firm and mean what you say. He'll either straighten up or walk away. Either way, the point is to let him know that he cannot treat you that way and get away with it. If you do not put your foot down, how will he know that what he is doing bothers you?

8. He uses passionate words and feelings. When men tend to lie, women are less able to catch it because they become so passionate and put so much emotion into their words. The reason why women get fooled into accepting the lie is because men do not usually express their emotions so

to seeing them be emotional and expressing themselves is new to the woman. He possibly could not be lying because he was so emotional. He was crying and you could really see and feel the emotion in his face. Never get fooled by this tactic. This is used by men when they feel really desperate. I'm not going to say that every time a man does it, it is a desperate ploy. What I will say is always look at the facts of the situation to so that you do not fall for his theatrics meant to distract you from the real truth.

9. He does the "sleepy act." Be very careful of the sleepy act. Men will try to use this when they have something to do or there is someone else they want to talk to on the phone. That is not to say this is the case every time. He might just feel like he needs some alone time. So the reason may actually vary but the intention will always be the same. He wants to get off the phone. So when a man starts yawning, he is saying that he is bored and wants to get off the phone. Usually, this will buy him a couple of hours or give you the impression that he is tired and wants some sleep. Remember there is no code book for men. You don't have to carry a decoder around. Men just use actions to say their words most of the time.

10. Be very careful around men that talk about their past a lot. Nine times out of ten, these men are freshly coming out of a bad relationship. This means that once they get everything off of their chest they tend to not spend as much time with you. A lot of women get hurt this way. The guy calls them off and on all day. They stay on the phone for hours and have really good conversations. The guy may spend time with the woman, and then all of a sudden, out of the blue, this guy changes his patterns. He doesn't call her as much. He makes excuses for why he cannot see her. Then it's like he starts to pick fights over anything. The woman is confused because she is wondering what

she did to make things change all of a sudden. Be careful of guys that talk about their past relationships a lot. He needs someone to talk to and once he has talked things out and felt better, then he will feel like he does not want to spend as much time with you anymore. Some guys are very unclear in their intentions and will have women around just to talk to them. So when you meet a guy that constantly talks about his past, do not get too attached. Do not feel bad thinking that you did something wrong. One reason he may not want to hang around you as much is because he may feel like he has told you too much. Once he gets his feelings out, he may feel embarrassed that he let out too much too soon. But, to spare your heart, never get attached to a man that tells you too much of his past. More likely, he just needs someone to talk to and may not be trying to keep you in his life permanently.

11. Sometimes men will talk to you to make another woman jealous. They may be mad at the other woman at the time and they want to talk to you to pass the time and let her know that they have other prospects. Usually, one of the signs is that he gets close to you really fast. He wants you to be honest and open with him. He tells you all of his whereabouts without you having to ask him. He's so open and honest that you completely trust him. This is not really a game. He is hurt and angry at the other woman that it causes him to cling to you to try to get off her. The only problem is once he recuperates and does not feel angry or hurt anymore, he will change. He will start to slowly push you away and distance himself from you, not calling you as much and even not being as open and truthful with you as before. He may even begin talking to the other woman again. Some men will still talk to you too because they may feel like it's good to have a friend in their corner. So you begin to feel like there is another

woman in the picture. There is. But what you failed to realize is he was only getting back at the other woman. That is why he gave you so much of his time. Now that he feels like the other woman misses and appreciates him, then that is when he does not give you so much of his time and slowly tries to break it off with you in so many words. How does he do that? By picking small arguments with you. This is to buy him some time. He knows that if he gets you mad, then you will not call because you are mad and it kind of gives him an excuse not to call you. Men get kind of cocky. He feels like everything is going good and he no longer needs you anymore, so he just does not watch what he says to you. Some men will use a fight to actually break up with you. The way that you know that he is trying to break up is if the fight was over something very simple and small. For instance, you might ask him a question and he just goes off and starts complaining of having no space. Or you may hug him and he gets up and acts like you are making him feel smothered. When a man starts acting weird and picking fights over small things, then he is actually saying that he wants to break up without even saying it. So the woman feels like it was her fault and she caused the fight when really that's what he was hoping would happen anyway. He just wants you to feel like the decision was yours or mutual, when really the decision was really his all along.

12. A man never gives you anything, not even on holidays or on your birthday. Basically he wants everything for free and won't spend time or money on you but once every blue moon. This man has someone and he is keeping you on the side for when he wants to see you.

13. He says that he does not want any commitment or relationship of any kind. He lets you know upfront that he does not want a relationship. He may even tell you that he

has been badly hurt or maybe he is going through a bad breakup. Basically this guy is saying that he only wants sex from you in so many words. He's letting you know upfront that his intention is just sex with you. Whether he has been hurt or not, the fact remains that he is only looking for sex. If you get involved with this guy, then chances are you will never be taken out. A date will be having sex and then watching a movie at your place or his.

14. He never wants to show you to his friends or family. And if you do happen to meet one of them, he casually introduces you like you're just an acquaintance. Actions do speak louder than words so don't wait to hear a man say that he's not that into you before you learn to see the signs for what they are.

All told, not all men are like the above, as each man is different. Some men do not care and will treat women the way that they allow themselves to be treated. If a man feels that he cannot use you, then nine times out of ten he will not call you anymore and he will move on. Sometimes he will give a reason and sometimes he won't. But either way, when you see signs of him disrespecting you, don't be afraid to move on to a guy that wants to treat you right.

THE MIRROR OF HAPPINESS

BE HAPPY WITH OR WITHOUT A MAN!

I hear some women say that they will begin to be happy once they lose weight or when they get a man. I say, be happy now and then when things change in your life, be ready for it. There will always be some kind of problem that will come into our lives. We all know that this life is not perfect. There is always going to be some kind of problem in life that you will have to deal with. It is not going to go away. Happiness is a reflection. Happiness can only be obtained in one's self. When you look in the mirror do you believe that you are beautiful? Do you believe that you have something to offer the world? If you answered no to either one of these questions, then I want you to look in the mirror again. Happiness is being yourself and being at peace with the way that you are. Happiness is a reflection with how happy we are with ourselves. There is no way that a man can give you what you don't have. You must find it in yourself and then others can see that reflection.

We have to adjust our attitudes so we can be happy with or without a man. Whether you're single, dating someone, or married, you will always encounter different problems. There is nothing wrong with being single, dating, or getting married. Don't fall into the trap of thinking that once you have a man, all of your problems will disappear and you can be happy. That is not the way life works. It's easy to think that being with another person will solve all our problems. I'm not saying that dating or being with someone will not bring you joy. But one of the causes of getting hurt in relationships is when we think happiness is found in another person and not in ourselves.

Maybe you are not happy with your job, or maybe there are things that are going on in your life. So you put all your energy into finding someone who will give you hope. That is when you set yourself up for a big fall. There are plenty of guys out there who claim to be looking for a relationship but who do not really want one. Some men are even looking for a woman to take care of them. Everyone's intentions are different. In a relationship, your intention may be to encourage and be there for him. However, the guy you're dating may just want someone he can regularly sleep with or another place to go to when his main girlfriend starts acting up. So if the relationship goes south, then your hope goes with it. So it's important to be happy before you get into a relationship so that your happiness is not determined by it. You can be happy with a man and without one. Also, sometimes when we are looking for happiness, we accept anything because we are so desperate to find what we are searching for. So we try anything and everyone. And the wrong man will see that and take great advantage of you. You stepped into the relationship sad but now you're depressed. So the relationship did not add anything to your life. Actually, it took away more than it gave.

I BROUGHT MY OWN JOY; WHERE'S YOURS?

What you want to do is bring your own amount of joy to the relationship. You want to love yourself for who you are. If the other person cannot accept this, then you should move on. Women must make a conscious choice to accept themselves for who they are—flaws and all. Changing will not help anyone in the relationship. In fact, I can guarantee that you will suffer the most. When we change to fit a man's ideal of who we should be, then we lose what makes us special. What if every woman in the world acted and looked alike? It doesn't take a rocket scientist to know that the world would be a boring place.

Twins who look identical have totally different personalities. Once you really get to know them, you can close your eyes and tell them apart based on their conversation. Twins who look alike do not act alike. This should tell us as women that we were never meant to be like another woman. We were created the way we are for a reason. There is an old saying that says, "Beauty is in the eye of the beholder." What that means is that there is a man for every woman. There is some man out there that will look at you and think that you are the most beautiful woman on the planet. What prevents women from finding their own uniqueness is that they take one man's standard and try to become the woman he wants. You are a valuable person that has a lot to offer the world. It's okay to be yourself and find something in life that makes you happy. It doesn't have to be getting into a relationship with a man or having good looks. It can be something so simple but wonderful like drawing, decorating, music, poetry, literature, gardening, teaching, fashion, crafts, business, and the list goes on. Once you find your own happiness that is not tied to a man, whether they leave or stay, you can continue to be happy.

Every woman is different so naturally each woman has to look at her own life and find out what is best for her. Just because you may see all of your friends married or in a relationship doesn't mean you have to entirely focus on that right now. A man does not have to be your entire focus right now, especially if he is not the right one. No man is worth trading your life and happiness for. You might say that it is hard to find a good man right now. You may look around and think everybody is in a relationship but you. Do not get discouraged. Wait for the man who will be right for you.

A GOOD MAN'S EXPIRATION DATE

What happens to a lot of women is they find a good man after they have dated all the wrong ones first. So they compromise and look for the least unpleasant man. And therefore he gets classified as a so-called good man when really the woman feels like he's the least of the worst from the bunch.

She may have settled because she got discouraged and thought, *This is the best I can get*. It's not that many women do not want a good man; it's just that they feel like good men either do not exist or have all died out by now. When you're hurting and angry, the pain blinds you from seeing a difference in men. It's easy to believe that all men are the same when your heart has not had time to heal.

Have you ever heard the phrase, "One bad apple spoils the barrel"? It is a true saying. Sometimes, it's easy to believe that being treated wrong by men is a normal thing.

This is what happened to a 30-year-old woman named Marsha. Marsha was an accountant who was making decent money working for a good firm. She was so used to all the wrong men that she eventually began to accept the idea that her perception of men was as good as it gets. She was basically the bread winner in her relationships. The men she became involved with did not have jobs or, immediately after meeting her, would get laid off or quit. She often said, "Being a successful woman made it hard to find a man. Men are intimidated by my success and are afraid to talk to me." She would pay for all the meals and all the dates that she went out on. She just felt that it was the new millennium and women could be just as independent as men. She wanted to be wined and dined by a man, but her success did not allow it. Eventually, Marsha become very serious with a guy named Greg who moved in with her after two months. For the first three months, everything was fine, but then Greg seemed to take over Marsha's place as if it were his. He would eat all of her food but wouldn't help her buy the groceries. He would drive her car without asking her, and when he returned it, the gas hand would be near the empty mark. He would leave his clothes all over her apartment and would make so many calls on her cell phone that different people would call her phone in the middle of the night. Greg had just been fired from his job from being late too many times and she did not want to insult him by being a nag. So she tried to put up with the situation as best as she could.

One day, as Marsha was in the grocery store picking up some groceries, she ran into a guy that she went to college with named Jamal. Jamal was a nice guy that always kept to himself. She didn't really know him personally, but they had taken a few courses together in college. Jamal had just finished his master's degree and was working at a local college in Academic Affairs. The longer they talked, the more she noticed that they had a lot in common. They liked the same genres of music and movies, and they both even had weird cravings for ice cream and nutmeg. Jamal asked Marsha if she would like to go out sometime to a movie or to dinner. He was paying if that was okay with her. Immediately, she felt uncomfortable. She was in a relationship, and she didn't know what to say. Jamal was okay, but she felt like he was just too good to be true. So she politely offered him a rain check.

On the way home, she couldn't help thinking about Jamal. He was handsome and hardworking, and they had so much in common. Greg, on the other hand, couldn't keep a job for more than a couple weeks at a time, but he was there for her when she needed him. Jamal would probably lose interest in her in a week. In a way, Greg made Marsha feel comfortable because he made her feel needed. They did not have the best relationship, but who did? Marsha decided that it was best that she stay with Greg. She knew that she had made the right decision. When she turned the key in the door, Greg was ready to go out to dinner. He had his suit on, and he told Marsha they were going to a very nice restaurant that night. He had found a job, and he was going to apply for it tomorrow.

Marsha should have jumped up in the air with joy, but instead she walked calmly to her bedroom and slammed the door. Greg didn't own one suit in the year that she had known him. All of a sudden, Greg was wearing a new designer suit that cost at least a thousand dollars. She didn't buy it, so she wondered where he had gotten it from. Lately Greg had been coming home in the mornings and she had even smelled perfume on him a couple of times. Marsha began to suspect that Greg was cheating on her with another woman, even though she felt like she had been the one that was there for him when he didn't have a job. Marsha thought more and more about Jamal. She had spent a lot of time and money in this relationship to blow it all away. So what if Jamal wanted to pay for lunch? Life was about more than a man paying for dinner. *She* could pay for dinner. Greg was the best thing that had happened to her. Her other relationships didn't last long because men felt insecure around her. Greg was comfortable with her success. He didn't feel intimidated when she paid for things. He always said all the right things when she needed to hear them. Jamal was a nice guy, but she just had to work on her relationship with Greg. Marsha sat down on the bed; a few minutes later, she heard the door slam. Marsha and Greg were having problems that no amount of money could fix. He started talking to her like she did not have any worth and everything made him upset. There was no amount Marsha could spend on him to make him happy. She could tell that he wanted to leave, but she did not know what she did to make him so miserable. All she could do is wait and hope that things changed for the better.

A year later, Marsha came home and Greg's stuff was gone. When she went to the bank to check her bank account, Greg had withdrawn all of the money from both her savings and her checking accounts.

SAY YOU NEED ME AND I WILL STAY

One of the things that help to keep women in bad relationships is dependency. Women like to feel needed. They like to feel that they have given their man something no other woman has. Marsha felt Greg needed her. Just knowing that someone wanted her was enough to keep her in a bad situation as long as she felt needed and wanted.

She felt she could offer Greg something that no other woman was able to. She was secure in their relationship because she felt he needed her. Other men were intimidated by her success, but Greg did not have a problem with it. In a way, Martha may have felt he would never leave because he was not intimidated by her being able to pay for dinner. In fact, he rather enjoyed that she could pick up the tab when he couldn't. When Martha met Jamal in the grocery store, she was afraid to talk to Jamal although they made a connection. Marsha believed that Jamal would probably lose interest in her in a week. In Marsha's mind, she wanted to be with a man that accepted that she was successful. Jamal seemed to scare Marsha because she was not sure how he would take her success. So although they connected, Marsha felt more comfortable staying with a guy that she thought would never leave than being with a guy that she thought would leave in a week. In the end, Greg left with all of Marsha's money.

Never stay in a relationship because you fear rejection from other men. Marsha could not move on to a healthier relationship because she was afraid. There is an old saying that says, "You never know until you try." What happens to most women is they become afraid to be with a new man because they fear rejection. The man that is not treating them right is consistently there in their life. He may not be portraying positive behavior, but he is "reliable and familiar." They condition their minds to believe that as long as their man's behavior is consistent, then it is okay if he treats them wrong. In other words, women may stay with a man that she feels is treating her bad but will never leave than a man that will not treat her bad but may eventually leave. Marsha may have passed up a great man because she was afraid to leave a bad relationship to find a better one.

PATTERNS TELL THE STORY

Maybe something like this has happened to you in some way. Maybe your experience was not as severe but it was harmful enough to make you mistrust men. Every man is not the same. One of the things that will help women when they are dating men is to look at his behavior. How he treats you in the beginning of the relationship is exactly how he is going to treat you during the relationship. If he talks down to you now, he will do it later in the relationship. If he is asking you for money now, he will do it later in the relationship. If he pesters your for intimacy in the beginning of the relationship, then he probably only wants intimacy from you. Real men get to know the person that you are first.

If he always makes excuses why he cannot see you, then he will continue that pattern later. Don't ever think that you can change a man because you can't. Don't tell yourself that he is like this now but then he will see what a good woman you are. The only person that you can successfully change is the one that stares back at you in the mirror. We can always decide to implement new thoughts and behavior patterns every day. All it takes is a choice and a will to change. Changing other people is not that easy. The human will is too strong to be controlled. It does not matter how much you think it will be a good idea. If someone doesn't want to do something, they are not going to do it.

So if a guy tells you upfront that he does not want a relationship, or that his ideas and views about what a relationship is supposed to be are different from yours, then think twice before committing to him. While opposites do attract, many times relationships go south because later on, both the man and the woman find out that the other will not budge from their viewpoint and beliefs.

A great way to avoid heartache is to ask questions when you meet the guy. This helps you get a feel for what kind of guy the man is. I'm not talking about interrogation—just simple questions about him and what he likes to do. For example:

1. What kind of movies does he like? This question tells you a little about his personality. If he likes comedies, then of course he likes to laugh and looks at life in a lighthearted way. If he likes action movies, then he's more into excitement and adventure. Scary movies mean that he likes a good scare. He likes to know about the unknown or he likes a good surprise. Epic or heroic movies mean that he likes films that have meaning and justice in them. He may be very big on how people treat him.

2. What is his family background and where did he grow up? A lot of times, just asking questions about his family life will tell you if he might have had issues with his parents. Many men who have issues committing to women never really knew their dads or were not very close to their moms. Just talking to him about his family life will give you some insight into any issues or insecurities he might have developed from childhood. Maybe he was always compared to another sibling who was more successful so he always feels that he has to prove himself. Maybe he was abused by his dad as a child, and he has anger issues that he has not dealt with. Asking these questions now can save you a lot of heartache later.

3. What was the longest relationship he was in? This gives you some idea of how he views a relationship. If he was never in a relationship longer than a couple of months, then he may see women as replaceable. As soon as he gets bored, then he is ready to move on to the next one. If a man tells you that he has been in long-term relationships that lasted anywhere from two years or more, then he is looking for a commitment. That said, just because a guy has been in long relationships does not in any way mean

that you should let your guard down and get relaxed with him. Get to know him, and let his actions and how he treats you determine his character.

4. How long ago was your last relationship? This question is very important. This gives you an idea of how fresh his last relationship was. If he says "three weeks ago," then you know that he might not be over his last relationship yet. Be careful because this means you may be a rebound. That's not to say that he will go back to her, but a lot of times when a relationship is started to get over someone else, then the woman ends up being hurt in the end. Is he genuinely interested in you, or is he just trying to get off of his last girlfriend? Take things slowly because you want him to decide if he has feelings for you or if he is just using you to move on. Does he really want to get to know you or is he just in a rush to get over someone? If he says it has been several months or years since his last relationship, then find out the reason why it ended. In the back of your mind, ask yourself, "Does this guy have trust issues with women? Or is he actually in a relationship and he's acting like he's not? Never rule out anything until you get to know this man.

5. What does he like to do? What are his hobbies? This question is important because it gives you a window into his soul. If a guy tells you that he likes to drink a lot and go to clubs, then you know that he is really just looking for a good time. He may not have any goals in mind at that point in his life and he sees life as one big party. If a guy tells you that he likes to paint, make things, work on cars, or some other useful hobby, then you know that he has something in his life that he enjoys doing. A lot of times, people take up hobbies to occupy their spare time or to do something they simply enjoy. The fact that he has something positive to do that takes up his time lets you

know that when this guy gets bored, he's not necessarily off to occupy his time with other women.

6. What are his religious beliefs? Make sure that you both have common interests in this area, because if you don't it will cause conflict later on in the relationship as you won't be able to agree and relate much to each other. Everyone feels like they can overcome anything once the relationship starts. Then as you spend more and more time together, it becomes apparent that the conflicting things that you once loved about each other start to become the root of your arguments. So it's important to get each other ideas and beliefs on the table early on in the relationship to see if they will be a problem later.

7. Ask him what kind of relationship he is looking for. Does he want a serious relationship? Does he just want sex? Or is he looking for someone that he can hang out with? These questions may seem unimportant. But you will be surprised how many women find out years into a relationship that men do not want to commit to them or carry their relationship further than friendship. Relationships can mean different things to different people based on their beliefs, experiences, goals, personalities, and family backgrounds. So never assume that just because a guy says he wants a relationship that everything's fine and that you should never ask him this question. If he says he wants a relationship, then find out what kind. Tell him what kind of relationship you're looking for too. That way, there would be no surprises or miscommunication later on. If he is not looking for the same kind of relationship that you want, then he will let you know. But trust me you'll rather know early on *before* you get to liking him than later when you already love him and he does not want to commit.

There are a lot more questions to ask but the above should get you started. One important thing to remember when you are asking questions is to remember what he tells you. The main way to find out if a person is lying to you is to ask him questions and see what he tells you. Then ask that same question again later and see if it matches up. Remember, facts do not change but lies do. Take for instance Jessie and Kathy's relationship.

Kathy and Jessie met on a dating site. Kathy was feeling pretty lonely and she became happy when she finally had the chance to met Jessie. Kathy was 29 and Jessie was 34. She had never been married, but Jessie was divorced. He didn't have any children, and he looked like he was a very nice guy. He talked about the Lord on his profile, so Kathy had a very good feeling about him. For their first date, Jessie took Kathy to a small restaurant so they could talk.

"So tell me. How long have you been divorced?" Kathy asked, while biting into her salad.

"It's been two years since the divorce. I caught her cheating on me one day when I came home from work, and since then I have not spoken to her." Jessie looked Kathy in the eyes and quickly tore off a piece of roll and began chewing it. Immediately Kathy stopped chewing and looked at Jessie for a long time.

"Are you serious? You caught your wife in the act with another guy?" Kathy looked apologetically at him.

"Right, it happens. You just have to move on and keep pushing," he said, while taking another bite of his roll. After moments of silence, Jessie finally looked Kathy in the eyes.

"You're right, this sort of thing seems to happen every day, but at the same time, I can't imagine how devastated you are right now." Kathy reached out her hand to touch Jessie's.

"Well, maybe I have found someone that will be different." Jessie smiled and squeezed her hand back.

Throughout dinner, the two talked and had a nice time. Kathy learned that Jessie had been married for years to his ex-wife before she started cheating on him. She became pregnant, but the baby was by the man that she was cheating on him with. His wife had already told him that before she left. Kathy also learned that Jessie married because he had been teased and rejected by women a lot. Jessie revealed to Kathy that the reason it took him so long to get married was because he had been hurt a lot and he had trust issues with women. Jessie told her that because of what had happened, he was not ready for a relationship and he definitely wanted to take things slow.

Kathy and Jessie began talking off and on over the next two months. There were times that Kathy could never reach Jessie, and he would return her calls either really early in the morning or late at night. And sometimes it would be a couple of days later. They could never talk very long, and Kathy was beginning to suspect that Jessie was still married and lying to her this whole time. When Kathy would ask if they could meet, Jessie always had an excuse as to why he could not meet her. He was either out of town or running errands for his mom.

At this point, Kathy became discouraged. She wanted to find love, but it seemed like most of the guys she met were either married or in a relationship. In the back of her mind, she believed that he was married, but at the same time she could not believe that he would go on a dating site if he was.

Kathy had to know so she made another account on the dating website she met Jessie on and did not include a picture this time. She messaged him and asked him if he was looking for some fun. She did not think that he would reply back, but surprisingly he started a chat with her.

JESSIE: Hey, what kind of fun do you have in mind?

KATHY: Oh, just looking to let my hair loose and have a good time. Any suggestions in mind?

JESSIE: Where do you stay at, dear?

KATHY: Hey, we just met. Lol I want to talk to you a little more and find out what you are all about.

JESSIE: Lol. What do you want to know? I'm an open book. Lol.

KATHY: On your profile it says that you are divorced. How long were you together?

JESSIE: We were together for three years and then she cheated on me with another guy.

KATHY: I'm so sorry. Did you catch her? How did you find out?

JESSIE: She told me after she had our baby that she was seeing another guy and did not love me anymore.

(Pause)

JESSIE: Hey you still there?

KATHY: I am—wow, how do you know that the baby is yours? Do you think it may be the other guy's?

JESSIE: Naw. It's mine. We didn't start having problems until after the baby was born. One day, I picked up the house phone accidently and heard them talking about going back to a hotel to have sex.

KATHY: What did you do?

JESSIE: The only thing I could do. I begged her to stay for our marriage and the baby's sake. We went to marriage counseling, but it did not work.

KATHY: Have you dated or talked to anyone since then?

JESSIE: No. Not since then. I haven't been able to really talk to a woman since she did that. I have trust issues with women. I was always rejected and cheated on.

(User has left the chat)

JESSIE: Hello.

JESSIE: Are you still there?

Like many women Karen felt betrayed after learning that the man she had gotten to know over the last couple of months had lied to her. The story he told her at dinner was not consistent with the story he thought he was telling another woman on the dating site. Be very careful and cautious of men that will say anything to evoke sympathy from you. I'm not saying that every man is like that. But be very careful of the guys that are because their main objective is to get what they want from you, whether it's money or sex. In Kathy's case, Jessie's story was different every time he talked to a woman. Kathy could only get in touch with Jessie at certain times. And when she wanted to see him, he always had an excuse.

Beware when you can never see a man. He may be spending time with someone else or he may even be married.

Signs of men that want to use you:

1. They never answer your calls. Instead, they will immediately text you after you call or just wait to return your call after a couple of days.

2. They do not like being asked many questions. Since they are lying to you anyway, then asking questions is a good way to catch them in their lies or for them to trip up and forget the lie that they told you. When the truth is told, you do not have this problem; lies, on the other hand, are so easy to forget because they are fabricated anyway. So asking questions and remembering what he said is a good way to catch him in a lie if you happen to ask him the question later on. That said, do not go looking to catch a man in a lie; however, remembering what he told you is important especially when you are just meeting someone you barely know.

3. They are too touchy feely when they first meet you. It seems like their whole intent is to get in your pants, and they want to hold hands, cuddle, and rub all over your

body—and you barely even know each other yet. There is a time and a place for cuddling and showing affection. But if this guy is doing this and you just met them, chances are he is just trying to use you and does not have good intentions for you.

4. The questions that he does ask you are related to your job, your car, and your address. Everybody asks where you work at or what kind of car you drive. But manipulators only seem to want to know this information and nothing else. They may ask a few questions other than that but their main focus is your financial stability. It's the first thing out of their mouths and the only thing that they want to ask you. They are not worried about getting to know you as much as they are about taking your money.

5. They want to rush into a relationship too fast. They constantly ask you about the other people you talk to and are often possessive. They are guys that do not mean you any good. They can be too controlling—as in, he wants to control your every move, who you talk to, and what you do. Or they could be trying to play games with you and use you to their advantage, whether it's for sex or money. Sometimes it's for both.

6. They want to know everything about you too fast. You want to tell the truth. The only thing that is risky is revealing information too much too fast. Manipulators look for any piece of information or insecurity to use against you. For example, if he knows that men have cheated on you a lot, then he knows that you may feel like men are not faithful and do not want you. So at first he will pretend to support you and encourage you, so that you start to depend on him or feel comfortable around him. And then, he will slowly begin to act negatively towards you and start making you feel bad all the time. What is so funny about this technique

is that someone actually has to tell you what he is doing to you for you to be aware. Don't reveal too much too fast. But, don't lie. Just say, "I don't really want to discuss that," or "Let's talk about something else." If he persists and does not respect your boundary, then ask him something really personal to change the subject. Manipulators do not like to give out personal information because they are all too aware that once you give out that information, then you're more vulnerable for attack. So in other words, they keep their guard up. The name of the game is to play you, not have you play them.

7. They are very humble in the beginning. When you first meet them, you will probably think to yourself that they are the most humble person you have met. They are always talking about what they can and can never do to a person. They do not want to be seen in a bad light at all, so they try to be as moral and as good as they can. They are very charming men. They are very intelligent and always seem to know the right things to say. They seem to have knowledge in psychology and they know how women think.

8. They always want to make everything seem like it was your idea. They are very good about portraying their ideas or thoughts as if they were yours in the first place. They want to give you the illusion that you are in control and calling the shots when really, they are moving you like a pawn in a chess game. For example, if they want sex from you, then they may make it seem like they do not really want that from you. They only want to get to know you. Once they feel you are comfortable and they have proven that they want something more from you, then they will contradict themselves and change their behavior. They may start talking in a sexual way or getting touchy feely. Then if their moves do not work and you question their

intentions, they place the blame on you. They find some way to twist it back around so that it seems like they are only doing what you want them to do.

9. They always know the right things to say. These men are very good at using women and know how they think. So he is going to be the type of man that knows what you want to hear and will say it. The only thing is he will say anything that you want to hear whether he means it or not. That's not to say that men cannot be considerate and thoughtful. But manipulative men are always positive and persuasive men. So if you find yourself always feeling used or manipulated into doing something that you do not want to do, then chances are that he is saying all the things you want to hear to get you to do what he wants.

10. They constantly talk about women and cuss a lot whenever they mention something about them. A man that is always telling you about his experiences with women is a player. He is constantly playing women and feeling bad about what he does. He cannot tell the women that he has hurt what he feels so he tells you to get it off of his chest. It may seem that he may actually be hurt off of these experiences. Since men know women are very caring and sympathetic, he may try to make it seem like it's always the women's fault as to why it did not work out. When really, he may be the reason why it did not work out. Be very careful because a man that can talk about women in this manner and always uses negative words to describe them does not have any respect for you or women as a whole. If he can talk about them that way, then he will be telling another woman about you if the relationship does not work out. And believe me, he will place the blame on you. A man's relationship and breakup history is a good factor in determining how he will treat you. If a man tells you stories of being with women that he never called back

or has slept with, then he is giving you a preview of how he will talk about you to someone else.

11. They brag about having skills in bed. A man that brags about majoring in sex is not a good man to be with. If that is his only accomplishment, then that means he spends most of his time getting women into bed. It also means that he does not have anything going for him. When that is the first thing a man talks about, that means that is all he has to offer. Some men will use sex to get women to buy them all kinds of things and to get their heads so messed up that they feel that they cannot be without them. Be careful around the type of man that says sex is what he majors in; don't stick around to know if he is telling the truth unless you're ready to lose a lot more than you have gained.

12. They suddenly become a different person. Usually these men will put on a good act until they get what they want. Once they become intimate with you or get what they want, then they will show you their true self. You might even feel like you are talking to a different person. This can happen within a matter of weeks or months; it depends on how soon this person gets what he wants from you. He may even tell you that he is a good person and he will do anything for anybody. Then the next sentence may be that he had been taken advantage of a lot. Be careful of someone who actually tells other people their weaknesses and insecurities on the first meeting. Usually, that kind of information comes out over a period of time and with trust. For him to say that right away means that he is trying to secure your trust. You have to understand that men do not do that when they first meet someone. Most women will complain that men never open up about what is bothering them or share enough. So what makes this man open up so soon about something so personal that

can be used against him later? The real reason he is letting go of this information is because he wants you to feel like he is opening up to you and sharing when he is not. His intention is to paint a false picture of himself so that you do not see his true self.

13. They talk for hours and hours on the phone. Most men know that women like to talk; thus, they feel they need to talk to them often to make them feel a big connection. Usually, men who talk for hours and hours on the phone are those that do not have a job or those who often play a lot of games with women. A man that likes to spend hours and hours on the phone will suddenly change once you become intimate with him. He may always have excuses why he has to call you back and become very silent on the phone whereas he was so talkative before. If he really likes to talk on the phone, then his behavior will be consistent. He will only probably become talkative once you talk about sex or money. So be very careful.

14. They are too obsessed with looks. This type of man will tell you about the women he dated in the past. He will try to play it like he was very picky back then but he has changed now. That is not the case a lot of the time. He is still obsessed with looks, but he may be trying something new because he felt like he could not use those women. The women may have felt like they were too pretty to pay for anything. So he may want to try to talk to someone who doesn't feel so pretty; such a woman will feel so thankful to be with him that she pretty much pays for everything. He might try to give you the impression that he is not trying to sleep with you. And he may be telling the truth in a way. His first intention is not to sleep with you. He wants to talk to you and learn your secrets without you being aware of it. So he will probably tell you that he likes honesty and doesn't want you both to lie to each other, so that you tell

him a lot more than you intend to. Manipulators know psychology so just telling them anything that might have been painful for you is a lot of information to them. Once he finds your weakness, he will play it for what it's worth and use it against you. He's not trying to sleep with you because his main focus is your money. And he may even be sleeping with someone else on the side. So be very careful when a man keeps talking about all the pretty women he dates and how he is trying something new. In this case, new doesn't always mean good.

15. They like to play sad cards. Men that want to manipulate you will always give you a sad story and will play on your sympathy. They will probably start their sentences off with, "I'm not trying to manipulate you or get you to feel sorry for me but..." Their main goal is to get what they want so a sad story helps to achieve this goal. For instance, they may want money from you. They do not want to ask you for money because they don't want you to see them as manipulative. So they may talk about how they never have any money. They may have child support that takes all of their money. But they do not mind because that is for their kids. But they just wish that they had some money to be able to buy you something nice. It makes them feel bad that they cannot do the same things for you like you do for them. After they see that it may be getting to you, they might feel safe to look at you and very gently bring up the topic of just borrowing a small loan to be able to get something to eat or help out with their bills, while adding that they are not trying to use you. Use caution. If he can ask you for a small loan, then eventually he will ask you for a big loan. Unless you're going to keep it up, then do not start it. When a real man cares about you, he does not take and take from you. But if a man does not care for you, then he has no problem doing this.

16. They don't do what they say they are going to do. They promise to call you at a certain time, but they never do. They may ask you for money and promise to pay it back, but there will always be an excuse as to why they cannot repay it. Manipulative men are good at promising things that you will never see the fruition of. A real man will keep his word. When you meet one that does not, get out of the relationship as soon as you can.

17. They never want to meet your friends and family. They want you to spend less and less time with them. The reason why they do not want to meet your family or friends is so that no one will see the game he is playing on you. In order for manipulation to work, then you cannot be aware of the game. That is why manipulators do not like you to ask them questions. They do not want you to figure out their game nor their motive.

18. They are often passionate actors. These men put so much passion into everything they say. They will look you straight in the eye and be serious and passionate about what they are saying. So they must be telling the truth right? That is not necessarily true. They are just really good liars that know how to give a persuasive argument to a lie. It can be argued the sky is really yellow and not blue if you use enough persuasion and you really believe what you are talking about. Even though we can see that the sky is blue with clouds in them, the right person can be so persuasive in arguing that the sky is yellow that you may start to rethink if the sky is really blue.

19. Manipulators don't like it if you think. Instead, they like it better when their women play dumb because this makes it easier for the men to take advantage of them. So instead of getting swayed by a man's lies, think about what he is saying and see if it makes sense to you. Most women have

intuition. We know when something is not right because we will get a feeling. Something will tell us that he is lying no matter how good the lie may sound. Manipulators will always try to convince you that you are being paranoid and that you are worrying too much. They do not want you to think because thinking leads to discovery. Instead, they want to stay in a state of denial about things. They want you to see things for what they are not. They want to make you think they are really in love with you and they are really trying to be a man who takes care of you. But really, they want you to take care of them.

20. Be careful of men that do not have any goals in life. Beware of men that have not had a job or a car in a long time and they do not have any reasons as to why they do not have one by now. However, there are men who prefer bicycles or commuting due to the environmental causes they embrace. And then, there are those who may have lost a job or a car due to the poor economy and struggling job market. Maybe he went through a nasty divorce that left him broke and in a helpless situation. These are understandable reasons versus a man that just does not want to do anything for himself and would rather use a woman to get what he wants instead of working for it. I don't care if a man has a dinted up car. A real man will have something. We all go through times when life gets hard and we might lose our job or we might be saving up for a car. Maybe our old car broke down and we are going through a time that we have to wait until we have enough money to buy another one. But a real man will have a car and a job. Look at his work history. Has he always had a job? Or are there a lot of gaps in his work history? This kind of man is lazy and wants a woman to take care of him. A real man has a job and has always had a job. Do not get me wrong; life does happen and there will be

times that all of us will be looking for work because the companies we worked for might have shut down or there were layoffs. But men that are not trying to use you will have a consistent work history and will not ask you for money. If a man has a job, but does not have a car, ask him how long it has been since he had one. If he says years, then run. If he says that it's been a couple of weeks because his car broke down, but he is in the process of getting the money to get another one or to get it fixed, then watch to see if it happens. But a man that has not had a car in years can mean either two things: (*a*) his license was revoked, or (*b*) he does not have goals in life and thinks things should be handed to him.

21. Manipulative men love to keep you laughing. They do not want you to be serious. They want you to smile all the time and take everything lightly. Laughter is definitely good for the soul. So laugh everyday if that is at all possible. But manipulators have a motive and purpose for wanting you to never get upset and always take everything lightly. Their main purpose is to be able to get away with anything that they want to do. They want you to develop a carefree attitude that allows them to do what they want to without you getting upset and calling them on their game. For example: Carla and Bruce had been dating for two months. Bruce would sometimes go out of town to gamble on the weekend. Carla would call his phone fifteen times, leaving messages for Bruce to call her back. When Bruce did call her back, it was always on a Monday. He said he was not able to call her back because the casinos did not allow phones or cameras within the premises. So he had to wait until he got back to call her. That did make sense but Carla wondered why Bruce could never call her when he got back to his motel room. Sometimes he wouldn't tell her that he was going out of town. Carla Carla thought

this was odd, but Bruce assured her that he was only gambling and that he tried to call her but she did not pick up her phone. When Carla assured Bruce that she did not receive a missed call from him, he began to get upset and tell her that he did call her. Bruce told Carla that he was tired of having to prove his innocence to her. She should learn to trust him and stop being insecure. He wanted her to think the best of him like he thought the best of her.

The issue with Carla at the moment was not trust; it was respect. She was not upset that Bruce decided to go out of town; it was the fact that he did not think enough of her to call her back when she called him, or at least return her calls so that she would not worry. If Bruce did not have anything to hide, why couldn't he call her back to let her know that he was out of town?

Many times when you cannot get in touch with a man while he claims he is out of town, he may be seeing another woman. Many women complain about not being able to reach their men when they go out of town. And the out-of-town trip is always spontaneous and at the last minute. A lot of men will use the out-of-town excuse when they are going to hang out with another woman and do not want you to call or hang out with them. That is not to say that every man who goes out of town is cheating, but if you never can reach him until he returns, then chances are he may be cheating.

22. They have fake issues. Manipulators share certain things about their life to make you feel comfortable in sharing yours. They may claim to have trust issues with women or rejection phobias from being rejected by a lot of women. I'm not saying that no man has experienced this. There are some men that *have* been rejected, but a manipulator will lie to get what he wants, whether it is true or not. The main key is not to make you paranoid of every man

that you meet. The key is to expose you to the different manipulation tactics that hurt women. Usually when a person is being manipulated, they can feel it, but they just don't know how they are being manipulated. So they are torn. They feel used, but they also feel like they cannot prove it and they are being paranoid. Chances are if you feel like you are being taken advantage of, then you are. Recognizing the tactics of manipulators will greatly help in avoiding being manipulated by some man that means to use you for his own benefit.

23. They are always upset. They always talk about how others had let them down or done them wrong. There are several things wrong with these men. They are very negative and do not know how to let things go. They like manipulating you into feeling sorry for them, and they like to play the victim role in order to evoke sympathy from you. Drop these kinds of men; they will only make you feel depressed, and the next thing you know you are picking up his habits.

24. They always have an excuse as to why they could not see you or buy you anything. These types of men only want to take from you and not give. Drop them as soon as possible because it is clear that they are users.

KEEP YOUR LIFE; ADD HIM INTO IT!

Another reason women can become hurt in a relationship is that they spend all of their time with a man. When the relationship is over, they feel that a piece of them is missing. Never put all of your time into just one person. When you do this, you set yourself up to be hurt. There is nothing wrong with spending time with men. Just don't spend all of your time with them so that when the relationship is over, you're in bed for a week, watching Lifetime shows, and eating gallons of ice cream. Invite men into your life, but do not change your life because they came into it.

You don't want to spend every waking moment with a man because once the relationship is over, everything will remind you of him.

That is what happened to Brittany when she met Austin. Brittany was a bright and intelligent twenty-four-year-old. She liked to work out every Tuesday and Thursday at the gym. She would meet up with her friends once a week for a girls' night out. Sometimes they went to the park or to book clubs. Whatever they were doing, the main goal of girls' night out was to laugh and talk about things that were going on in their lives. She also liked to attend Wednesday night Bible study after she got off from work. You could often find her shopping for CDs because she liked to listen to classical music and jazz. She played the piano and the violin which she loved to play in her spare time. While she was on her way home from a workout, she caught a flat tire on her way home. When she got out of her car, another car pulled up beside hers and rolled down the window. To her surprise, a guy who looked to be around twenty-four asked her if she needed any help. The guy helped her get a spare tire on the car. While they were talking, they found out that they had a lot in common. They set up a date.

Austin and Brittany began to spend a lot of time together. Brittany's friends no longer saw her for their girls' night out and she stopped going to Wednesday night Bible study. Austin didn't like jazz or classical music so Brittany stopped buying those CDs. Austin liked pop/rock and R&B, so Brittany spent her free time looking at CDs for Austin. When her friends would call her to hang out, she would decline. She would not leave the house until Austin called to say he wanted to hang out. If she did make plans with her friends, she would cancel them if Austin called. Her family and friends complained constantly about not being able to see much of her anymore. She even stopped working out on Tuesdays and Thursdays to make more time for Austin.

Brittany did feel guilty that she saw her friends less, but she had a man. She really wanted to make this relationship work, and she was so happy. Five months into their relationship, Austin began to feel smothered. He liked spending time with Brittany, but lately he felt like they had been spending too much time together. His feelings began to change towards Brittany, and he wasn't exactly sure how he felt about her anymore. He felt he needed some time to really get his thoughts together. Austin told Brittany that he wasn't really sure of his feelings for her at that point. He thought that they should take a break for a little while. Brittany was heartbroken and sad. Her feelings had not changed for Austin. She was hopeful that Austin just needed a little time and he would really see that he cared for and loved her. Austin did keep in touch with Brittany occasionally. After a couple of weeks, she learned that he was seeing different people.

Brittany was still very hopeful that Austin was just exploring his options. She was very confident that once he dated for a while he would see that she was the only one for him. After a couple of months, Austin confided in her that he was seeing a coworker he worked with. Brittany could not hide her hurt feelings. She became depressed. She no longer hung out with her friends or family. Instead, she would sit in the house watching TV and eating ice cream. Brittany gained fifteen pounds after she had learned Austin was dating a new girl. She stayed in the house unless she had to go to work. A couple of times, she called in sick to work. She was devastated. She wondered how Austin could do this to her after all that she had given up for him. Most of all, she was upset that he waited five months to find out his feelings for her had changed.

Eventually, after about a year and a half, Brittany began to get back into her routine. She began hanging out with her friends and family and even started to work out again. She rejoined her Bible study group on Wednesdays and even played a couple of solos on the piano and her violin at church. After three months of exercising, eating healthy, and changing her eating habits, she began to lose the weight she had gained after her breakup. Four months later, Brittany began dating again. This time, she did not change her schedule to accommodate the new guy in her life. She made time for him, but she did not change her whole lifestyle. She still works out, meets up with her friends once a week, and spends time playing the piano and violin. She still continues to do things that she likes, but she also has fun spending time with Marcus.

TREAT THE NEXT RELATIONSHIP DIFFERENTLY

In Brittany's relationship with Austin, she stopped doing the things that she liked to do. Her life revolved around him. You should never give up your world because someone new walked into your life. You can share the things that you love to do with them, but never let them take away your happiness. It took a while for Brittany to get over Austin. She became depressed because she had placed all of her happiness in Austin. Before they met, she found happiness in other things. But then she began to believe he was the source of her happiness. So when her source of happiness left, she didn't know how to find joy without him.

It took a long time for Brittany to get over Austin. What brought her out of her depression was the fact that she found her joy again. She found happiness that was not connected to just being with a man. Also, she did not get into another relationship right away. She waited until she was internally happy before she decided to date again. A lot of times, women will get into another relationship still sad and hurt. What this does is it makes the wound bigger. Every time the new man hurts you, it's just going to make your open wound sting more. Take the time to let your wound heal before you get into a new relationship. This ensures that you have had the proper time to recover. That way, the new guy is only judged for what he does and not for any pain any other man has caused you.

When you have a chance to heal, you are able to think of positive things instead of negative ones. When you first break up with someone, it seems like you will never laugh again. Healing and moving on lets you know that you are stronger than you think. You can make it and do positive things in life. There is hope after a broken heart. After a broken heart, we can learn to use that negative energy and produce positive energy. You can do this by making a conscious choice to do so. It doesn't take a lot of energy to just sit there and hurt. It takes all your energy to get up and keep moving, although it hurts. It's not going to be easy the first day or the next. But it gets easier when you keep practicing it. Sometimes you will be tempted to think that this person was the beginning and end of your life's happiness. That is not true. Yes, this person did bring joy into your life. But your happiness does not end with them.

Brittany could have put her life on hold waiting for Austin to come back to make her happy again. But no, she made a conscious choice that she was going to regain her happiness again. Brittany learned from her mistake with Austin. She remembered with the next guy to keep her life and invite him into it.

HOW MEN SHOW THEY CARE

I've heard a lot of women ask, "How do you really know when a guy likes you?" Just like those women, I was curious so I went to my library and looked it up. The rules said bizarre things that seemed contrary to me. One of the rules mentioned that he would stare at you at lot. He would not know what to say when he was around you. He would act shy and he would try to act like he did not like you even though he did.

But these rules do not mean that a guy likes you. Most men that really like you may be shy, but they will approach you and try to talk to you about anything. And most importantly, they will want you to know that they like you because they are interested. However, every man is different. So I'm not going to say that every man is going to act the same. But one thing I do know is that when a guy is interested in you, he *will* let you know.

But like other hopeful women, I wanted a guide that would help me get a man. Contrarily, the books only left me confused and heartbroken. It was only after I started to look back at my past relationships that I learned that men are not that complicated. Men are actually very simple. You can tell a man really likes you when he shows you that he cares. He compliments you and uplifts you. If you're feeling bad about one of your flaws, he shows you instead that that flaw is ones of the traits he loves about you.

He doesn't pressure you to do anything you don't want to do. A lot of relationship books will tell you to make the man wait long enough but not too long because he will lose interest. But when a man really cares about you, he can wait. When a guy doesn't really care about you, he can leave if you're not willing to become intimate. A lot of women choose to have sex much earlier than they planned to in a relationship because they think that if they don't, the guy will leave. In some cases, this is the truth. He will leave because he is not really trying to get to know you. He's only after one thing. A real man will tell you that you both have time. He'll get to know you before moving on to the next level.

NO PARTS SOLD SEPARATELY

When God made women, he made them with body, mind, soul, and heart. Some men like to rip women off and love only one part of a woman when she is made up of many qualities. Some men will try to make you feel like your body is the only thing that gives you worth. That is a lie to steal your self-esteem so that they can manipulate you to their advantage. Remind them that you have a mind and a heart and they are connected to your body. Your body has no parts that can be "sold separately." If he wants one specific part, he has to want them all.

When a man cares about you, he goes out of his way to show you in the little things that he says and does. He sees your inner beauty before anything else. You can wear flip flops and jeans that have holes, but he will still think that you look beautiful. Of course, he'd like to see you dressed up once in a while, but he can still see you're beautiful even when you're not trying to be. When a man cares about you, he will show you it in how he treats you. He will open doors for you or pull out your chair. He will never hit you or talk down to you. He is not ashamed to show you off in public. You don't just go to his house and watch TV all day. He introduces you to his family and friends. He wants everyone to know that you are his girl because he is so proud and happy to be with you. When a man cares for you, he listens to you. He knows even the smallest things about you that you didn't even know he noticed. He thinks of creative ways to show you that you are special to him.

Most men will not be able to tell you how they really feel. For some, they find it hard to express their feelings verbally. But even though they may not be able to express how they feel, they will show you in their own way. They may write you a poem, draw you something beautiful, make you something out of wood, buy you a gift that does not cost a lot (but took a lot of time and listening skills to buy). You might have pointed out a necklace that you saw in a store six months ago, and for your birthday, he surprises you with it. When a man really cares about you, he will make you feel special even in a room full of women. He will be loyal to you and he will stick by your side throughout the sunny and stormy days of your relationship. If you tell him you are pregnant, he will take on his responsibility instead of changing his number. He will not have you working two jobs to support him while he is sitting at home. He will not leave you after you have become intimate with him.

Most importantly, a man will not treat the woman he cares about wrong. He will not be just a taker. He will not ask you for money and he will not depend on you financially. He will not use inappropriate language around you because he thinks highly of you. He will be careful of the places he takes you. If a man takes you to night clubs and places where drugs and drinking are rampant, then he definitely does not care for you.

If a man ever speaks of inviting people in to have sex with both of you, then this man does not care for you at all. What true man wants to share the woman he cares about with other men or other partners? If he proposes this to you, then he does not care for you or think highly of you at all.

There are a lot of women out there that have been giving since day one in their relationships. They have done all the giving and yet they have never received anything back. When a man cares for you, he will give *back*. He will get you things for your birthday, and he will want you to have nice things because he thinks that you are special and worth it. I'm not saying that gifts are everything or that they have to cost thousands of dollars. What I am saying is that there should be a fair amount of giving and receiving on both ends. If you look around your room and can only see a used cell phone case he let you borrow and a CD he made for you, then he has been the one taking without giving anything back, especially when his room is filled with things that you have given him and yours has nothing from him. Basically what I am saying is that when a man cares for you, he pays for things. He does not say he cannot pay for any of your meals or he does not have any money to buy you a birthday present. If you are in a relationship with this kind of man, then exit immediately because this type of guy does not care for you and is only looking for handouts. A real man will not be afraid to show you that he cares through his actions or his words.

Real men will tell you that they love you through their actions and words. They will not lead you on. There are a lot of men out there that will tell you they love you but not mean it. But you can tell if a man means what he says through his actions. Unlike words, actions never lie. A real man, when he says he loves you, is not tied to a motive. He feels for you because he cares about you and there is something special about you.

A real man will impact your life in a positive way. You're not going to have to bail him out of jail every six months. He is not going to give you drama every night and make you wonder if he is cheating on you with another woman. He is going to build the relationship on trust, honesty, and friendship. A real man will not have an indifferent attitude about you. Some men will call you every three or four days and think that is okay. Then they get upset when you want to talk to them for more than five minutes. I'm not saying that a real man will spend three or four hours on the phone with you every night. My point is that if he wants to talk to you, he will find ways to fit you into his schedule. You are a part of his life and he cares for you. Any man that acts like he is doing you a favor by calling you does not care about you.

Be aware of a man that can never spend time with you. It usually means that he is seeing someone else and you are just a side option. A real man wants to spend time with you and will not have an excuse as to why he cannot see you. There will be times that you cannot see each other. But his pattern will be consistent. Always look at a man's pattern; if there is any inconsistency, then he does not mean you any good.

If you do not take anything else out of this book, then do not ever forget this: a real man will show you how he feels by the way he treats you. Real men do not treat the women they care about wrong. They treat them like they would treat someone that they love and respect. So if a guy is treating you any other way, then his talk is cheap and you should move on.

NO TRANSLATION NEEDED

Some relationship books will try to make men seem really difficult to understand. They make it seem like the male species are a foreign race and you would need a translation guide to understand them. The best way to understand a man is to get to know him. Spend time with him and take the relationship slow. One thing women mistakenly do in the beginning of a relationship is to give their heart too fast. If it's only the second date and you're thinking about marriage, please slow down.

Observe the man's behavior before you give your heart to him. It will detour you from a lot of hurt. If he's not really taking the initiative to spend time with you in the beginning of the relationship, then it will not happen later. Do not try to make him fall for you or change yourself to make him like you. Just take the date as a new experience and move on.

NOT EVERYTHING IS CODE

One thing to stay away from in a relationship is code breaking. What most relationship books will tell women is that men speak a different language. They will have you feeling like you need to carry a code book around to understand men. That is not true. When I read relationship books, there is always some kind of code to break. If he said this, it meant that. A lot of times, some women ruin good relationships by constantly trying to break codes that never were coded. If a man says that he is hungry, that's all it means. He is just hungry. When he says he is tired, he just needs some sleep. When he doesn't want to talk about his feelings, then it only means he is not in a sharing mood. Do not worry. When he is ready, he will come and talk to you. Just give him some space, and he will come to you after he has thought it out. Everybody needs a little space. No one likes to feel pressured into sharing anything before they are ready. Just think how you would feel if the guy pressured you to become intimate before you were ready. You would probably want him to respect your boundaries until you felt you were ready.

It is very important to understand that men do not speak code. But they will give you subtle hints if they like or don't like you, just like women give men little hints to let them know how they feel. But there is no code about men that you have to stress yourself out trying to break. One of the biggest questions I hear women ask is, "How do I know if a guy likes me or not?" The answer to this doesn't require code breaking of any kind. If you are out with a guy and he does not call you back within the next couple of days, then it means he's not into you. If you call a guy all the time and he never calls you back, then he's not into you. If a guy says that he will call you but does not, then he's not into you. And he was probably trying not to hurt your feelings or felt cowardly about coming right out and telling you that he didn't feel the connection. I will admit that some men lie. But a lie is not a code. A lie is a lie. A lie means that he is a liar. It does not mean that men speak a foreign language that women cannot understand.

Once a woman learns to read a man's actions, it will then eliminate the confusion about the misconception that all men send mixed signals or are hard to understand. If a guy cares about you and likes you, then he will show it. If a guy does not care about you and does not have good intentions toward you, then he will also display that behavior. So the question is not how to read the code in a man's conversation but how to tell the difference in his actions—how a man shows he cares and how he shows he doesn't.

The only way to really get to know a person is to spend time with them over a period of time. You don't have to know everything about a man on the first date. There are going to be some expressions that you do not understand. There are going to be some behavior patterns that are going to take a little time to get used to. Over time, you will learn them and understand that these traits are just part of him. Remember: men and women think and act differently. For most women, they would have no problem expressing their emotions. But some men have to internalize a situation in their heads before they share their feelings about it. They may want to make sure they have all the information first.

The best way to break down barriers is to keep in mind that everyone is different. Try not to get too sensitive before you have actually learned a man's personality and behavior patterns. When a man reacts differently, it is easy to believe he does not care. That is not always the case. Men also have different experiences and personalities than women. So quite naturally they are not going to react to every situation in the same way that we would. That is okay. Do not get too upset. The areas he is weak in might be your strengths. The areas you are weak in might be his strengths. So don't try to compete, but instead learn to work together.

ACTIONS SPEAK LOUDER THAN WORDS!

We have all heard the saying, "Actions speak louder than words." What that means is that sometimes, the best way to get your point across is through actions. For instance, the timeframe that a man calls you represents how much respect he has for you. If you tell him not to call past 10 p.m., then he should respect that. If he calls you after the time you have given him, then he does not respect you. Don't try to pick up the phone and tell him to please call you before 10:00 p.m. Just do not answer the phone.

When he calls you back the next day to ask why you didn't return his call, tell him that you do not answer calls after a certain time. If he really likes you, he will respect your request and learn to call you at an appropriate time. If he doesn't, then there are more fish in the sea. Always remember: how a man treats you while you are still getting to know each other is an indication of how he will treat you during the relationship. If he doesn't think enough to call you at a decent hour, then he doesn't mean anything good. He just wants to see what you will let him get away with.

I've heard some women say that this is the new millennium and it's nerdy to tell a man to call you before 10:00 p.m. It's really not. One of the reasons women get so hurt in relationships is that they stop asking the man to respect them. He figures if you do not respect yourself, then why should he? If a man really cares about you, then he wouldn't treat you badly. Something is wrong when he has all day to call you but he waits till late night to do so. When a man calls you really late, then that means he is bored or he only wants you to come over to his place for sex. He is not trying to get to know you; rather, he is only trying to get you into his bed. A woman can decipher a man's intention toward her by how he treats her and when he calls her. A guy that has all day to call you but does it late at night, only to ask you to come to his place or inform you that he wants to come over to yours, does not care for you. When a man cares about you, he wants to show you off in public in full daylight, not at night when most people are sleep.

Look at a man's actions as well as his words; they should both coincide together. The common misconception that confuses a lot of women is when a man's words are different from his actions. If a man is truly into you, then you do not have to play guessing games. His actions will be clear and connected to what he is telling you. Also, be very careful if the only time a man makes time for you is to have sex. You plan to go to a movie or out to eat and he always makes excuses as to why he does not want to go. But when it comes to having sex, there never is an excuse.

Never give a man too many excuses because excuses hide the truth. You can say that he works a third shift and that is why you never get to see him. But the truth of the matter is, he can spend some time with you—if he really wants to. You don't have to see him every day, but he will make some time in his schedule to see you. If he doesn't want to see you, then he will use that excuse as to why he cannot see you.

Common excuses men use when they do not want to see you:

1. "I'm really tired. I think I will go to bed. I have to get up early in the morning." This means that he does not want to talk to you and he feels that you are not getting the hint.

2. "I'm going out of town tomorrow." This means that he hopes that you do not call him because he has already told you that he is going to be out of town. He may feel that you want to see him and this buys him some time from having to see you.

3. "I'm running errands for my mom/sister/aunt." This isn't to say that a man will never run errands for his mom. But this is a common excuse that a man will use when he does not want to see you. I'm not sure why men do this, but it is always a woman in their family that they are running errands for. It will never be their dad or their brother. It will always be a woman.

4. "I have to go see my grandmother or my grandfather today." Usually men will use this one when they want to end the date early or if they are just not feeling you. "I'm doing something right now but maybe we can hang out later?" This means that he does not want to spend time with you. Later usually means maybe you can come over to his place later and have sex. Be leery of men that only want to spend time with you at night but have no time

for you during the day. Usually, when men keep making excuses as to why they cannot see you, it means that they have rethought being with you and have decided that they really don't want to be with you. Most men do have a conscience, and will not want to play with women's emotions. If they are not feeling you, then they prefer not to do anything to give you mixed signals. Men that do not care will sleep with you anyway, as that is all that they wanted. They will have sex with you and then dump you as soon as you get too clingy. The length of time that they'll allow you to be in their life depends on how clingy you get. Sometimes men get caught up doing this. The woman starts to complain that the guy never spends time with her and thus threatens to leave. It seems like he really doesn't care, and then weeks or months later, he calls her again. She thinks that he just couldn't take being without her anymore, when really, he just misses the sex.

5. When he does return your call, it is late at night. And he makes up excuses as to why he has to get off the phone early. He really does not want to talk. This just means that he wants to keep the communication lines open. He may not have gotten what he wanted from you yet, so he's just trying to act like he cares a little until he gets what he wants.

6. "I'll call you back." If he sounds irritated or in a rush to say it, then he definitely does not want to talk to you. Don't worry because a man that is not trying to get to know you is not worth thinking about either.

7. "I'm a homebody. I don't really like to go out." That means that he doesn't want to do anything with you other than have you come back to his place. Be careful of this man because for all your dates, you will be sitting at the house.

Homebody really means that he is not trying to take you out and he does not want to spend any money on you.

A man's actions must coincide with what he is telling you. If there is a conflict between the two, then reevaluate your relationship with this man. Obviously, he is not telling you the whole truth. Do not feel dumb if you think back over situations and you say to yourself, "Why on earth could I not see this?" Don't beat yourself up over it. When you are in a bad situation and you feel lonely, you're really looking for a friend. You see the signs but you are still hoping that there are some caring men out there. You hope that things would change, and that he would see that you are a good woman and would then change for you. Don't hold your breath on this idea. There are some instances when men do change and learn to appreciate you when that was not their intention before. But this is rare.

A man knows, upon meeting a woman, if he wants sex, friendship, or a relationship with her. But he does not tell the woman these thoughts until much later in the relationship. He likes to wait and see what happens before he predicts or acts on things. Since he does not rely solely on his emotions, he waits to analyze a situation, especially if it may possibly involve something deeper. And in analyzing it, he gives the situation more time. While the woman complains that the man seems to be happy with the way things are and doesn't seem to be making an effort to make the relationship grow, the man feels more like letting things happen naturally. If something doesn't happen naturally, then it was not meant to be.

I LOVE YOU; IT SLIPPED, WHAT SHOULD I DO?

There has been a lot of debate about when to tell a man that you love him. It seems like every time a woman tells a man that she loves him, he starts acting funny and does not want to spend any more time with her. Why is that? The answer is very simple.

Men are taught by society to be in control of their emotions at all times. It seems like there is an unspoken code that men can not cry and express their emotions as openly as women. So when you tell a man that you love him, then it automatically causes him to withdraw to see if he really loves you. Men often need to have some alone time to see how they really feel about you. It's not at all easy for them to let their feelings out, unlike women. So that is why it seems like every time a woman tells a man she loves him, he withdraws. Often, if the guy feels like his feelings are mutual for the woman, he may hide it a little longer because he does not want to feel vulnerable or make it seem as if the woman can take advantage of him. Society considers emotions in men as a sign of weakness, so if he does not express them back right away, do not get scared. Just give him some space and let him think things through and he will come back around.

When a man does not love you back, then that would push him away. And that is the same for women. When a man tells a woman he loves her and she does not love him back, then that is going to push her away because she does not feel the same way that he does. Never keep someone in a relationship by using guilt and manipulation. Be honest and straightforward and always give a man a choice in how he feels. If he feels like he does not love you back, then at least respect him for being honest with you and for not playing with your emotions. Some men will use women knowing they do not love them. So weigh it out. Would you rather have a man be honest with you about his feelings and not use you or pretend to love you just to get the things he wants from you?

Give him some time to see how he feels about you. Maybe over time he will grow to love you. Let him come to that decision without any pressure from you. If it turns out that you are at two different places and you're not going in the same direction with your feelings, then sit down and have a talk and see where the relationship is going. This is when you should come to a compromise or some kind of agreement.

I'm not going to give you some rule that tells you when the right time to say "I love you" is. Each person and relationship is different. But I will say that you should not tell a man you love him after the second date. Wait a while to be sure that what you are feeling is real. Say those words when you feel them and when you think you're ready. But always remember that when you say it, you shouldn't expect them to say it back right away. Never try to push your feelings on someone. Say what you feel and mean what you say. Give the person some time to see how they feel. Always note that when you tell someone you love them, it's to express an emotion, not a manipulating tool to get the guy to feel something that he doesn't.

MORE FISH IN THE SEA

Don't take excuses from a man for mistreating you. You have value and it is worth standing up for. Linda learned this the hard way with Thomas. Linda believed that a woman should be firm but also very understanding. She grew up in a single-parent home and she promised herself that one day she would get married. Linda was looking for a guy that would marry and provide for her. She didn't want to seem desperate, but time was running out for her. She was almost thirty. Linda was so happy to have found a man that she let a lot of things Thomas did slide. Sometimes Thomas called her really late, knowing she had to get up and go to work in the morning. Linda didn't want to mess the relationship up so she did not say anything to Thomas about it. As time went on, Thomas began to schedule their dates later and later. Sometimes the date would be 9:00p.m. Sometimes he would take her out at 10:30 at night. This really upset Linda because Thomas had all day to see her but he would wait until late to meet with her. Linda kept her mouth shut because she did not want to say the wrong thing and be without a man.

Thomas would begin to say inconsiderate things to her like "Are you gaining weight?" "Why don't you do something to your hair?" or "You don't dress up anymore."" Linda was starting to feel very discouraged. She wanted to get married one day, but she did not want to be with a man that treated her like she was crap. She had to make a choice. Was a man worth this emotional abuse? She began to get depressed because she wanted to stay with Thomas, but she did not want the emotional abuse. She knew if she did not say anything, then she was giving him permission to keep doing it.

Finally, Linda made up her mind that she was not going to let Thomas treat her like she was a doormat. When he called her late at night, she did not answer the phone. When he scheduled a date very late at night, she would decline. When he would say inconsiderate things to her, she would tell him to take her home. She began going out with her friends instead of seeing him as much. Soon Thomas began to call Linda at a decent hour. He no longer took her out late at night. He even began to compliment her on her outfits and hairstyles. She no longer felt that she had to appease Thomas at her own sake. She could demand respect and still have a man too.

Linda was so afraid of losing Thomas that she did not demand respect from Thomas in the beginning of the relationship. She thought that if she spoke up, then he would leave. Anytime a man leaves because you demanded respect, then say "Thank you God!" Sometimes the best gift in life can be a no-good "dog" leaving and saying good-bye. Though you may hurt at first, he may have actually done you a huge favor in the long run. Thomas probably did not know that he was disrespecting Linda. He thought it was fine to call her late because she never said that he couldn't. She never complained about him picking her up late at night, so he kept doing it. When a man does something that offends you, let him know in a firm way. If he cares enough about you to change his ways, then work out your relationship. If he does not change his ways, then let him go. You self-respect is worth more than a no-good man.

NEVER TAKE LESS

Also, do not fall into the trap of thinking that you have to accept just anyone because time is running out. A lot of women are with men right now because they do not want to be lonely. No one wants to be lonely. Everybody wants to be with somebody that makes them feel special. But when you are with someone that makes you feel unspecial, then you should let them go. Anyone that does not encourage you to reach new heights in your life shouldn't be there. Let me ask you a question. What if I told you I was going to give you a thousand dollars! Would you take it? There is one condition. You have to wait five years to get it. That means that you cannot withdraw it from the bank until the five years are up. If you do, then you can only get two hundred fifty dollars of the thousand. Sounds like a no-brainer until you really think about it. How many times have you settled for low quality men instead of waiting for a high quality one because you didn't want to be lonely at the time?

A lot of times, we settle for a man because we think we may have missed our chance. We lower our standards by thinking this is all that we can get. Life is too short to be unhappy. If you want joy in your life, sometimes you have to give joy to receive it. Do not wait to be with a man before you can be happy. If you do not have a man right now, then that is okay. While you are waiting, why not go to a movie with your friends? Or you can volunteer at a homeless shelter or a daycare. Take your niece or nephew out for lunch and a movie. Spend time with your family or plan a "me" day to pamper yourself. Read books or take up a hobby. While you are waiting for a man that is going to treat you right, fall in love with yourself. The worst thing that you can do in life is to ask someone to love you. Beat them to the punch and show them how it is done.

Veronica was twenty-six years old. She always pictured herself as a person that was nice-looking. She liked the fact that men always stared at her because it made her feel pretty and confident. Veronica had been on a lot of dates with men but for some reason her relationships did not last long. Men did not really have anything to offer her. They all asked the same questions and pretty much used the same lines. She wanted to be with a man that could give her something no other man could. She wanted excitement, enjoyment, adventure, and creativity. Lately, she had become depressed because she would be thirty soon. She wanted to experience the kind of love that would sweep her off her feet.

Veronica began to date different men than the ones she was used to dating. She was used to dating good-looking men with successful careers. Veronica decided she would try to focus more on personality than looks.

On one particular date, Veronica met a man named Sam, short for Samuel. Sam was the type of guy that believed life was very short and people should make the most of each day. He was very happy to be going out with Veronica. She was very pretty, and he couldn't wait to get to know her. Sam took Veronica to a very nice restaurant where a waiter seated them at a table. Whenever Sam asked Veronica about herself, he'd notice that she would avoid the subject. He'd ask Veronica about what she liked doing, and she would talk about the different men that she had dated. He was beginning to become very bored with her. He knew more about her past boyfriends in that last thirty minutes than he did about her. Finally, Sam put his head down on the table. Veronica was so startled; she began to nervously sip on her champagne while looking around the restaurant. When Sam did raise his head, he looked at Veronica for a very long time before speaking.

"Veronica, we have been here for almost an hour and you have not told me anything about you. I know most of your boyfriends by now and I do not know one thing about you."

"Samuel, haven't you been listening to a word I said? I have been telling you about the trips and things I liked to do with the men I dated."

"Well…Veronica, that is what I am talking about. You told me about your experiences with men but you never told me what you liked to do before you met them." Veronica tilted her head a little and opened her mouth and then closed it.

"Well, let's start over. Let's start with something easy. What is your favorite color?" Veronica thought for a minute and then replied that it was pink.

"Okay, good. We're off to a start. What is your favorite food?"

"That is an easy one. When I went to New York with Nick, he got me to try...I mean, I like seafood."

"Okay, we're getting somewhere. Now I'm going to ask you a harder question. Ready?"

"Ready." Veronica smiled at him.

"What did you like to do before you met these men and really traveled? What was your life like?" Veronica quickly dropped her smile. After five minutes of silence, Veronica finally spoke.

"I didn't have one."

EXCUSES JUST WON'T DO

Don't use the excuse "I'll get a life as soon as I get a man." Or, "I'll be happy as soon as I get a man." Or, "As soon as I get a man I'll find out what I like to do." Don't ask someone to do what you can do first. Waiting on a man to make you happy is like sitting in the same chair, from Monday to Friday. That is the same way life is. You can't say that you are going to meet a man on Tuesday. You never know when that special someone is going to come in your life. Be on the lookout, but don't keep yourself to a boring routine. Have fun also while you're waiting.

Don't make the mistake of waiting until you find a man before you find out what you like. When you came out of your mother's womb, life began. It didn't start when you met a man, and it doesn't end just because you don't have a man. It keeps going regardless of their presence or absence. That's not to say that you won't ever feel good around a man or become happy. What I'm saying is do not let a man control your joy.

DETOUR: TAKING ANOTHER ROUTE

What I'm about to say next is not going to be very popular but it must be said. Most of the time, we are not going to have our way in life. Life is filled with disappointments and detour signs that cannot be avoided. When you reach a detour sign, you do not sit quietly and wait for it to move. No, you would grumble first, but then you would start looking for another way to get to your destination. Why? Life does not stop because we came across a detour sign that wasn't in our plans. Sometimes these signs are going to suddenly pop up in our lives. We are going to have to be prepared for them when they come. Finding a man can be compared to reaching a detour sign. When we first fall in love, no one plans on a breakup. But they do happen. When it happens, it's easy to just want to stay at the detour sign until the bad dream is over. That's when life will prove to you that it can wait longer than you can. You can sit and wait for someone to come back, or you can move on with your life. Because whether they meant to hurt you or not, the truth is that not letting go only poisons your heart and keeps you from ever being happy or in love again. You always have those memories that stop you every time you want to be happy.

Nobody likes detour signs. It seems like they take longer than just going your usual way. Men can seem the same way. The man you were with was just fine. You became so used to having him around that you became comfortable with the old route. Now that he is gone, you have to take a detour. This detour seems so uncomfortable and you find a new route.

The old saying says, "The best things in life are worth waiting for." That is a true saying that still applies today. It is important that we do not become so hasty that we learn how to wait. We must learn how to take those detours when they come. When we see detour signs, then that means we must find another route to happiness. Don't keep a man around because you feel like a bad man is better than no man at all. A good man could be around the corner. You cannot receive something new if you are not willing to let go of something old. A lot of times that means waiting without a man to find a good one.

CAN THAT BE DONE?

Is it really impossible to be without a man for a little while? I know it seems like everyone has a man. Valentine's Day comes around and it may seem like you are the only one without a man. Christmas rolls around and you are the only one without a man. Your birthday rolls around and you are the only one without a man. That is not true. There are still women out there that are not scared when they come across a detour sign. They are lonely for a season, but loneliness does not always last. Sometimes a woman can become burned out from being with the wrong men. That's when she needs some rest before she gives away her heart again.

We all go through periods in our life when we do want companionship and we just don't want to be alone, but being in a wrong relationship is not better than being happy but alone. Having the wrong man in your life because you are tired of waiting is like asking for a depression pill. At first, you will appreciate it because then you finally have someone to talk to. Then you will notice more and more differences in the way you both think and act. Finally it will seem like you argue about everything. You'll find yourself quickly losing your joy. Once a manipulative man thinks that he has you right where he wants you, then he will really change to his true self. And if you thought the beginning of the relationship was bad, you haven't seen anything yet. He will take you through so much drama, that when another guy comes along, you do not want to see or hear anything from that new guy at all. He could actually be a good guy. But you can't see that because you've just been through too much. That is how some women lose out on meeting a good guy. They get impatient. They pick up anything. And then when the good man comes, they tell him they can't take any more men in their life right now.

There is nothing wrong with waiting for someone that will be different from the "dogs" that you have been with. Remember a good man cannot be with you if he sees you're still in a relationship. Many women miss out on good men because the detour sign scares them. They would rather stay with a no-good man than to move on without a man at all. Never place yourself in that situation. Always be willing to move on and look for something better. Even if it means you may have to wait before the right one comes along.

WAITING TAKES PATIENCE

This is what Sarah had to do. She had to wait for some time before she found a man that she wanted to be with. She was thirty-three. She felt that she might have missed her chance with love. She wanted the right man to accept her two lovely children into his life too. She had experienced relationships before that left her and her children heartbroken. Every time her children started becoming attached to the new guy in her life, he would then decide to leave. Finally, Sarah decided to focus on her children and stop dating for a while. She wanted to be married one day and she didn't like the fact that those dates never lasted long. She just wanted to meet a guy that wanted a serious relationship that one day might lead to more.

Sarah was really discouraged because a lot of men ran when she said that she had two children at home, aged ten and twelve. She hated it that her children didn't have a consistent man in their life. She hoped one day she would find the right man. A year and a half passed, and Sarah was getting impatient. She had met a man named Rob, but she really did not feel like he was the right one for her. She did not want to make that leap with Rob without the assurance that he would be there for the long haul. Whenever she brought up marriage, he was quick to tell her that she was moving too fast. Sarah thought moving in together was also moving too fast. Rob did not understand that Sarah had kids and she wanted to set a good example for them. Why would he take a large step to move in but not want to get married? She felt if he was not ready to get married, then he should take things slower and give them time to grow. In Sarah's heart, she felt like Rob was not really committed to a family life. But she was becoming lonely. So Sarah kept silent and began to date him off and on for two years.

After two years, Rob was still uncommitted to the relationship. He spent time with the kids occasionally, but he was still hassling Sarah about moving in. She felt like Rob did not respect her wishes. It seemed like he was only looking out for himself and not how it would affect her kids. Sarah decided that she was wasting her time with Rob. It was better to be lonely and happy than in a relationship and miserable. It was hard, but four months later, Sarah broke it off with Rob. She did not hear from him after that. Two years went by and Sarah was thirty-seven and single. She had lost all hope. She just made up in her mind that she was going to be single for the rest of her life. A couple of weeks later, Sarah met a man in his late thirties. She had met him while they were picking up their kids from school. The guy's name was Greg. He was a divorced single dad who was looking for a serious relationship. Greg wanted to get married again, but he wanted to take things slow before he made the leap. Sarah and Greg found out that they had a lot of things in common. They began to get serious about each other. They both respected the fact that the children might not have been ready for such a new and drastic change. So they dated for two years and in their third year, they decided to get married.

If Sarah would have accepted the fact that Rob was all that was out there, she would have missed out on Greg. Don't get so used to having a man around that you begin to believe that that is the standard norm. Being treated as if he really does not care for you is not acceptable. Rob was okay with being with Sarah without making a commitment to her. Do not be afraid to leave an old relationship for something better. It does not matter how many years you have been together. If he is not respecting you, then you need to let him go.

DON'T THROW AWAY THE PRIZE

How many women do you know let go of good men for all the wrong ones? Some women meet good men but they keep waiting for their old love to come back. They do not realize that they are facing a detour sign and must move on. So they make every excuse in the book why the good man is not their type. He can have a job and a car; pay for meals; spend time with her kids; call her on a regular basis; and want to spend time with her, but she will still say that there is something about him she doesn't trust, or that there just isn't any chemistry between them. On the flip side, the guy that she has chemistry with mistreats her and does not care about her at all. The next time you see her, you find a new mark on her and she says that she fell down or was being clumsy. He does not have a job or a car and he never buys her anything. He asks her for money and you see him with other women. When you try to tell your friend, she gets mad and says you're jealous.

It's not that your friend doesn't really want a good man because she really does. It's the fact that your friend has become so used to being with the wrong men that she doesn't know how to be with a man that really cares about her. She has become conditioned to being with these "dogs" that she feels that is all she can get. The "rescue me, anyone" syndrome could also apply to this situation. Your friend has been rescued. The guy that rescued her does not care about her at all. To her, it doesn't matter that he does not mean her any good. All that matters is that he was the first one to rescue her when she needed to be saved. So when any other man comes to save her, he does not get any credit because someone has already been there before him. So in her mind, the first person that has saved her is the hero, regardless of how he treats her.

Some women get so used to being treated bad that they do not understand that they are not supposed to be treated this way. When a man comes along that treats them with respect, then it catches them off guard. They do not know how to take this respectable behavior; they feel that is not how a man is supposed to act. Remember they are only going by their experiences where they have been poorly mistreated. It can happen to any woman. That is why it is very important not to settle for less.

How many times have you compromised your beliefs and what you felt was right just so that a man would hang out with you? Did you pay for meals, buy clothing and watches, and pay bills? If you answered yes, then I want to tell you not to beat yourself up. Life is a learning experience. But please note that a mistake is not something that we keep making. If a guy really cares for you, then he is not going to have you do all the work without him making an effort too. I encourage you to stop spending your money on him and ask him to step up and be a man. There is nothing wrong with doing things for someone you care about. But when you find yourself paying for things and feeling tired from doing so, then it's time to stop.

When you see them do a little, it's then that you do a little too. Don't do so much for a man to the point that the relationship is not a partnership anymore but a financial dependency. The only thing about this relationship is that you have invested time and money into something that will never be paid back.

Don't beat yourself up and think that you are stupid and that these things deserve to happen to you. I'm telling you these things so that you are aware of the changes that you have to make in certain areas of your life. I'm not judging you nor am I trying to make you feel bad. I am only trying to make you aware of how the game goes when a man feels like he can use you. The most important thing to remember now is that everyone makes mistakes. Sometimes experience is the best teacher because it makes you wiser and stronger in the end. So don't look back on the past, but examine your mistakes instead. Look back to see what you did wrong and move forward. You deserve to be happy. But in order to get there, you have to keep going.

GAMERS: ALWAYS IN GAME MODE

Be very careful because some men will play the good guy role. They will tell you all that they do for people. They may even pay for the first two dates to catch you off guard and make you think that they are not after your money or that they don't have any kind of motive. These men want to know everything about you so that they can know how to use you. If he spends a lot of time on the phone with you in the beginning, be careful because he is trying to use you. He will stay on the phone with you for two, four, or five hours trying to get enough information to know how to use you. A lot of women complain about men changing their habits. They complain that the man used to stay on the phone with them for hours in the beginning of the relationship but can barely spend twenty minutes later on. He didn't change. He meant to spend more time with you in the beginning to learn you and once he learns you then he feels like he knows you well enough not to have to stay on the phone with you. The wrong men will only get to know you to take advantage of you. Most of the time, they want to know how to get into your pants or they want money. Whatever the reason, there is always a reason.

Be careful of a man that can be sensitive one moment and irritable the next. Start watching his patterns. When is he the most irritated with you? When does he treat you nice? Chances are he treats you nice around payday or when he wants sex. At another time, he is irritated with you and his real emotions about you are surfacing. We all have stuff in our lives that make us a little more irritable than normal. Users and manipulators are irritable because they're faking that they like you to get what they want from you. So before you pay that bill or do anything for a man, be sure that you're doing it from your heart. Later on, you may discover that while it was a relationship for you, it was a game for him all along.

Ever dated a guy that took you out on a couple of dates and never called you back again? That can really lower anyone's self esteem. Then you started moping around the house because you really liked him and did not understand why he did not call you back. You wanted to call but you did not want to seem desperate or you called and he didn't return your calls. Well, most guys do not call back for three main reasons:

1. They just weren't into you. If they do not like you, they will not use you, unlike some guys without a conscience. They didn't feel a connection, so they just did not call. They prefer to let you down easy by not coming out and saying it outright, but their actions will tell you that they are not interested. Ladies, this is not code. So don't feel that men are hard to understand. If you're not feeling a guy and you do not want to hurt his feelings and you're not trying to use him, do you continue communication or do you stop calling him?

2. They wanted to use you but felt like they couldn't, so they did not call you again. Users, when they feel like they cannot use you, stop calling. Some people look better walking away then they do walking into your life. So a lot of times when a guy does not call you back, don't feel too bad. You might have just dodged a bullet.

3. They already have another woman. When men talk to you while they're still with other women, it may be because they have issues. They may have just broken up or they just couldn't deal with the situation any longer. So they attempt to move on. Most of the time, they are trying to prove a point to their girlfriends that they can get someone else if they really wanted to. But usually, once the relationship recovers or their girls apologize, the men will put you on the backburner. Only two-faced men try to date two women at a time. Most men will either cut ties if they decide to stay with their women. Or, they will not initiate phoning you but will answer your calls. Most

of the time, men do not know how to say "Please stop calling. I'm with someone." So they slowly stop answering calls or do not pick up as much when you call, hoping that you would get the hint.

THE CALLS MONTHS LATER

Do not be deceived. When you have not heard from a man in a couple of months and he suddenly contacts you, he may be on the rebound. This means someone may have broken up with him and he is in a desperate search to talk to someone to make himself feel better. Some women complain that men they have broken up with will call months later after the end of the relationship, wanting to get back together. I'm not going to say that some men are not sincere, because they may actually be. Sometimes though, many men who have been dumped may just be browsing their phonebook trying to find someone that will help them move on quicker. So be very wary because if the relationship did not work out the first time, then it was for a reason. And a man's patterns tell the story. Is he going to be the man that leaves and comes back to the relationship any time he wants to? The answer depends on how many times you let him. Take, for example, the case of Holly and BJ.

Holly and BJ would break up and get back together off and on for a period of five years. They were together for a year and then broke up for eleven months. Then they got back together for five months and broke up again for three months. Then they got back together for a month but decided it was not going to work. So they took a break for four months. BJ begged Holly back and they dated on and off for the last three years.

A man knows if he wants to be with you or not. In the dating stage, there shouldn't be so much confusion and instability. All couples will have fights and say things that they regret later on. But an off-and-on relationship is a sign that he is not consistent and isn't sure if he wants to be with you for the long term. He wants to know that you will always be there when he wants you, but beyond that there is no guarantee or commitment that he is looking to give you more than months and years here and there.

HOW MANIPULATORS GET IN YOUR HEAD

Users like to ask you a bunch of questions to find out how they can expose your weakness or insecurities. The answers to these questions in turn help them to get inside your head. But you shouldn't get to the point in which you get intimidated by a guy who asks you a question. Everyone asks questions. Normal questions when you first meet someone are:

1. Where are you from? Where did you grow up?

2. What was your major in college?

3. Do you have any children?

4. Where do you work? (If they start asking how much you make and where all you family members work, then they may be after your money).

5. Do you drive? (Most men want to know that you are not going to use them and that you have your own transportation. When he asks you several more questions regarding your car, then he is trying to figure out how many more payments you have on it, and how much money he can get from you every month since you may or may not be paying a car payment.)

6. Where do you live? (If he asks you too many questions about how much your rent is or if he can come over, then he is trying to use you. Everyone comes over to each other's apartments, but users want to come over when they first start talking to you. You do not know if this guy is a psycho or not. That is too fast. Be very careful.)

7. What's your favorite movie or book?
8. What's your favorite color?
9. Do you like sports?

When the questions start to get deeper than the ones mentioned above, then get very leery. Users love to use psychology to get inside your head and expose weaknesses that help them use you. Most manipulators are very good at seeming like they understand women and are very positive and encouraging. But when you really get to know them, they are very negative and condescending. Their favorite thing to do is get inside your head to point out everything that is wrong with you. Sometimes they may point out a trait that may have some truth to it. For instance, maybe you have a tendency to worry too much. A manipulator will take that trait and add on a bunch of other negative traits to make you feel like you have a very big problem. Manipulators look for insecurities, faults, or anything else they can use to criticize you. You will never hear them say anything negative about themselves, but they are always approaching others with negativity and finding fault with others. So do not let a manipulator fool you into thinking that something is so terribly wrong with you when really, they are the ones that have the issues.

Brad and Cinda met at a bar one night. Everything went well when they talked so they exchanged numbers. Cinda found Brad to be very romantic and he seemed to be in sync with her every thought without her having to tell him anything. He would always spend hours with her talking on the phone, asking her questions about her job, her family, and her life. He was interested in knowing everything about her. Cinda had never met a man like him that cared so much about her and wanted to know her every thought. Was she in heaven because he seemed so perfect? One night, after two weeks, Brad started to change. He would become irritated with her when she tried to express her opinions or talk about her thoughts. He would cut her off and start arguments about everything. Cinda was confused. How could he be so sweet and sensitive one minute and then be rude and impatient the next? Cinda decided to call Brad and talk about what was bothering him. Was she doing something wrong? Was it work? Was it financial matters? Cinda just needed to know what was wrong. She really liked Brad and wanted to make the relationship work.

BRAD: Hello.

CINDA: Hey, what are you doing? Are you busy?

BRAD: Naw. Just chilling and trying to stay cool.

CINDA: Hey, I think we need to talk. I have been feeling like something is bothering you and you're not talking about it.

BRAD: Nothing is bothering me. Why do you think something is bothering me?

CINDA: Well, lately you have just been really snappy, and whenever we talk, you start breathing a lot. We don't talk as much as we used to and I just want to know if I did something wrong.

BRAD: Baby, you did not do anything wrong. Everything is fine. I apologize if I might have done anything to make you feel that way.

CINDA: Okay. I feel better know. So do you want to do something this weekend? A movie? Dinner?

BRAD: I don't really feel like doing anything. It's just too hot to do anything right now. I have pretty much seen all the movies so there is nothing that I really want to see.

CINDA: Well, do you want to go to Starbucks and talk over tea and cake?

BRAD: You don't listen, do you? I just said that it was too hot to do anything and you're still trying to make suggestions.

(Silence)

CINDA: Well, I just wanted us to spend time together. Excuse me for not realizing that dating and chivalry belonged in ancient times.

BRAD: I don't mind spending time with you but you never listen and you always want your way. If I'm not doing what you want, then you get mad. I cannot spend all of my time with you. I get tired of that it gets on my nerves.

CINDA: I don't expect you to do what I want. Wanting to spend time with someone is not a lot to ask for. Why would you even say something like that?

BRAD: I get tired of arguing with you. Why do you do that? Why are you always negative and why do you have to make something out of nothing?

CINDA: I don't always make something out of nothing.

BRAD: You have to learn to let the past go. I think differently from most people. I move forward not backward.

CINDA: Brad, why are you talking to me like this? I didn't mean to start an argument. I'm sorry.

BRAD: I mean, that is just what you do. I've learned you. So it really doesn't bother me because I've gotten used to how you are. But sometimes I just can't deal with how you are.

CINDA: So what are you saying? You want to break up?

BRAD: I didn't say that. See, there you go jumping to conclusions. How do you come up with these ideas? What goes on in your head?

CINDA: Well, you're the one saying how bad I was and how you just can't handle me. So that's why I figured you wanted to break up.

(Silence)

BRAD: Nobody is talking about breaking up. We are just having a conversation. I'm just talking to you and trying to tell you all of this to make you feel better. If there was something about me that you didn't like or couldn't handle, then you would tell me right? Well that is all that I am doing with you.

CINDA: Brad, you make it sound like I am a bad person.

BRAD: You make me feel like I'm a bad person! You're always saying we need to talk because I'm acting this way but maybe there's a reason behind the way I'm acting.

(Silence)

CINDA: So what are you saying, I cause you to act like that because I nag you too much?

(Silence)

BRAD: Look, all I'm saying is just give me a little space; that is all. Everybody acts differently and most of the time, I'm busy doing things and trying to help other people. So when I get home I'm worn out and just need to relax.

CINDA: Well, I didn't know that I was bothering you. You don't have to worry about me calling anymore.

BRAD: If that is how you feel, then I can't stop you. I like talking to you but if that is what you want then fine.

CINDA: Brad, I wouldn't even feel that way if you didn't always make it seem like you did not have any time for me."

BRAD: Baby, I'm not used to having to give my women that kind of attention. I mean, I cannot spend every moment of my day with you. I have a life. If you did more stuff, then you wouldn't be so clingy. But you don't really do nothing so you would not understand.

(Cinda hangs up.)

BRAD: Hello? Hello? Hello?

What was the whole phone call about? The phone call for Cinda was about finding out what happened to the sweet, sensitive Brad she knew before. How could he have changed from a sensitive man to an insensitive one in just a matter of weeks? I'm not saying that Cinda was perfect, but when a man changes like that in a matter of weeks or days, then that is a sign of the game—the manipulation game to be exact. He spends his every moment learning you and he may stay on the phone for hours to do it. Once he learns you, then he knows how to manipulate you. When he knows how to manipulate you, then his real self comes out and that is when he does a total 180-degree change on you. He was always like that; he just didn't have enough information at first to really let his true self come out yet.

THE KINDS OF MEN OUT THERE

You are going to meet a lot of men in your life. Every man's personality will not be the same. You may see patterns in different men like cheating, lying, and having mood swings, but you will meet a lot of different personalities. Some will be good and some will be bad experiences for you. You will meet men, and it will seem like you go from one extreme to the other. But it's like you will meet a very cheap man and then you will meet a man that spends everything that he makes. You will meet a man that comes across to people as very dumb and then you will meet a man that has an IQ of a genius. It's like men are either really cheap or really foolish with money. There are too much into their looks or do not care at all. You may meet a man that is very sensitive or very insensitive. You will find more of what I am trying to say by reading the brief personality descriptions below. I want you to at least have some idea of what to look out for in each personality:

1. Confused Man—This man does not know what he wants to do with his life. He knows what he wants but he never seems to do anything to help himself achieve his goal. He waits on others to give him the things that he should be out getting himself. His lifestyle reflects that he is not going anywhere in his life. He dates different women and does not really know what kind of woman he truly wants. He is very impulsive and makes decisions based on his emotions at the time.

   What to look out for: In a way, this man will act like the woman in the relationship. He wants you to pay for everything. He wants to be wined and dined and given expensive gifts. He might even withhold his affection from you until you pay for things. Be very careful of this man because his goals and aspirations change so much from one minute to the next. He doesn't really know what he wants out of life so you cannot look too much into this kind of man. It's good to be in a short-term relationship with this man. Stay friends with this man because he does not know what he wants out of life. Everything changes with his emotions.

2. Driven Man—This man is very focused. He knows exactly what he wants out of life. He has goals and dreams that have not changed since he was a little kid. He will probably tell you that he has known what he wanted to do with his life since he was thirteen. He is not lying to you. He is very serious and is being absolutely truthful with you. This is the kind of man that will not let anything stand in

the way of his being successful or the accomplishment of his dreams.

What to look out for: This type of man does not have a sense of humor at all. He is very serious and does not know how to laugh. This does not mean that he is abusive just because he is serious. This man will need a woman that can make him laugh and show him how to laugh at himself. Don't expect this to happen overnight because it will not. So if you are with this type of man, just know that he is serious and you will have to work with him in the relationship to get him to see that you have to laugh in life.

3. Comic Man—This man is a little kid although he is in a grown man's body. He does not take life seriously. Instead he laughs through life and wants you to laugh in life too. Everything is funny to him and he cannot be serious for one moment. It's not necessarily a bad thing until you need him to really take life seriously. This is the type of man that will spend his whole life savings on video games and comic books. He enjoys life and believes in having fun.

What to look out for: This type of man is a little late on paying the bills on time. It is hard for him to be responsible because he stays in kid mode a lot. You will have fun with this guy but he will need a woman that doesn't mind him being playful. He also needs a serious woman that can balance his personality. He can teach her how to laugh and she can teach him to be responsible and how to be serious at times.

4. Controlling Man—The name speaks for itself. This man does not want you to do anything without his saying it. He wants to control how you walk, what you wear, how you talk, how you wear your hair, and even what you believe. If he thinks that something is not a good idea, then you are not allowed to do it. You will never have to work another

day in your life with this man, but if you have a mind of your own, then he is not for you.

What to look out for: There are some women out there that prefer men to make the decisions for them. They don't mind at all that their man controls what they say or do. There is somebody for everybody, but I honestly believe that if you are a headstrong woman that doesn't like having a man control you, you shouldn't get in a relationship with this man. You will constantly fight all of the time and arguments might turn abusive or get out of control.

5. Passive Man—This guy is a peacemaker. He does not like conflict in any form. He does not mind you not agreeing with him just as long as you both are not arguing about it. He values other people's opinions and he is very respectful. If you are looking to get a fight out of this guy, then you won't find it in him. If you force him to argue or go against his nature, then you risk losing this guy and being shut off from his life entirely. That is not to say that you will never have a disagreement with this guy. You will disagree from time to time, but your arguments will not be a big deal.

What to look out for: It may come across to many women that this guy is weak, but he is not. He just does not like confrontation. It takes a lot for this guy to get mad, but once he does, he can become cold towards you and he will not let you back in his life very easily. This guy is more into connection and respect than confrontation.

6. Radical Man—This type of guy will make an argument out of everything. He likes a great debate and does not like to take orders from anyone. He is not necessarily a bad guy. He just believes in standing up for himself and even others if he sees he can win the argument. He feels angered by injustice and will take any side just as long as he thinks he will win the argument.

What to look out for: If this type of guy is hurt from past experiences and relationships, then be very careful of him. His objective is to argue with anyone who picks a fight with him, and he will want to win. Everything will end in an argument. It does not matter if you apologize or not. He will fight you either way especially if he feels attacked. Be very leery of this type of guy, especially after he has been hurt. His attack is through his words which can be very hurtful.

7. Showboat Man—This guy is the type that is a snitch to put it nicely. He tells everyone's business, including his own. He will tell your business in a minute, especially when he is around a lot of people. His whole persona is about showing off. He is flashy and he feels a constant urge to boast about what he has.

   What to look out for: If you have confided any personal information to him and later on you fight, you can be sure that he will tell your secrets to his friends, his family, and even strangers. Do not tell this guy any information that you would not tell others yourself. He may not mean to show off and be as open with people, but when he gets to be around other people, he can't help but do exactly that.

8. Secretive Detective Guy—This guy is the opposite of the showboat guy. He does not let loose any information. You can tell this guy your deepest, darkest secrets and it would go with him to his grave.

   What to look out for: On the flipside, it is hard to get to know this man. He does not let anyone in because he trusts no one. You can know this man for five years and be able to get more information out of a stranger. It is okay if you share your business with him but do not expect him to share anything with you. He will never tell your secrets, but you will not get any either. If you are trying to get close to this guy, he will never let you in no matter how long you've known him. The relationship can work just as long as you're not trying to invade his personal space.

9. Picky Man—This man is extremely picky about the women he dates. He wants perfection to say the least. If he finds any flaws in you, then he will immediately end the relationship. The reason can be something as trivial like incorrectly filed fingernails or a crooked pinky toe.

What to look out for: He is constantly searching for the perfect woman and you will get hurt if you try to change this man. He may actually like you even though you are not perfect, but in the back of his mind he will never be able to commit to you because you do not meet his expectations. This man may sleep with you and even have meals with you, but all the time he is thinking how you repulse him. So eventually he will make excuses as to why he cannot see you. He may never tell you the real reason why he cannot see you because he feels like he will hurt your feelings. But do not be surprised if he tells his friends and it gets back to you through them.

10. No-Standards Man—This man is the opposite of Mr. Picky. There is no woman that he will not talk to. He does not care if she has flaws or if she does not comb her hair or if she smells. He will date this woman and stay in the relationship faithfully. He is not desperate. It may seem hard to believe, but he is not. The difference between no standards and being desperate is choice. The desperate guy feels as if he has no choice and he has to accept anything that he can get. The no-standards guy has choices but he prefers to be with the woman he gets involved with.

What to look out for: Once this man is involved in a relationship, he is faithful to the woman that he chooses to be with. If she ever dumps him, then he will find someone else to be with. But if she ever wants him back, no matter how bad the situation may be, he will go back. That also goes for when he is in a relationship with you. For some reason, this man may not have any standards in the type of women that he dates, but once he gets involved, he is very loyal. If she wants him back, he will leave you. If she dumps him again, he will come back. If she decides to pick him up again, then he will leave you again. It is a continuous cycle and she never loses her hold on him. So before you get involved with this type of guy, be very careful.

11. Passionate Man—This man is passionate about everything he talks about. He can talk about a stick of gum and make you feel like it is a human being. He tends to be very emotional, but only when it comes to subjects he cares about. You can almost say this man is an "actor." This man is not trying to run games on you; he just feels so passionate about everything.

   What to look out for: Try to avoid arguments with this guy; he will always win unless you are very passionate too in the way you discuss topics. What you will probably get tired of is how he turns simple topics into a big issue. Every issue is big with this guy. Unless you are a drama queen then you will get tired of this guy after the newness of the relationship rubs off. At first you will be amazed how a guy can be greatly emotional about things. Then you will just get tired of him being so emotional on every subject. What is so funny about this guy is that he will get dramatic over the way they put toothpaste in a bottle, but when you ask him how he feels about your relationship he will be calm and collected in his answer.

12. Numb Man—This man does not get overly excited about anything. This guy just seems to be going through the motions. He does not do anything with any enthusiasm or emotion. He is very calm in the way that he handles things and rarely does he show any emotion. You may see

an emotion pop on his face for five seconds and then it is quickly gone.

What to look out for: Something happened in this man's life to get him to this point. He may not have shown a lot of emotion before but maybe it was more than what he is actually showing now. These types of men tend to sleep a lot. They move very slowly and they prefer to sit a lot. You almost feel like this man is depressed, but he will deny it if you ask him. He will probably say that he is just a mellow guy.

13. Flirtatious Man—This man loves to flirt. He loved leading women on and seducing them. His main goal is to get women in his bed. He has many women in his life who he feels are just friends.

What to look out for: He may even be married or have a girlfriend while he flirts and seduces other women. This man does not let himself become attached to just one woman. He may care about a woman, but this man does not give his heart away to just one. It is the thrill of the chase and the seduction that he mostly enjoys. That is not to say that in marriage or a serious relationship, he will not be faithful. But he may have periods wherein you may begin to have suspicions about his faithfulness. There will always be a woman out there that he is attracted to. If this man cannot flirt, he may even become depressed until he is able to flirt with many women again. Most women complain of another woman. With this man you never have to worry about just one woman because there will always be many.

14. Faithful Man—This man believes that there is only one woman for him. He believes in being faithful and working hard. You can mostly find him doing his hobbies, working, or spending time with his family or with you. He will have a conversation with other women but he will never lead

them on. He will always tell them that he is married or in a relationship. This guy is a great guy to be around; he believes in love, trust, and faithfulness. And he will be that way in marriage as well as in the dating stage.

What to look out for: There is nothing that you really have to look out for in this guy. But this type of guy does not really see people's real intentions because he is such a loyal and faithful guy. So he sees the good in everyone. This is not a bad thing. But his attitude of trusting people and not seeing their true intentions may drive you up the wall. You may find it hard to convince this man that he has to watch out for people who have bad intentions against him because he will not believe you.

15. Liar—A liar is someone who does not tell the truth. They consistently lie about everything because they feel that if they tell the truth, it could ruin their plans. Liars want to get things out of people. It may be money, it may be sex, or it may be sympathy. Their main objective is to get what they want by twisting the truth to ensure that they get what they want.

What to look out for: Do not believe that liars ever tell the truth. A liar will always twist the truth, and their stories change much too often. They are quick thinkers, so even if you catch them in a lie they know what to say to get out of it. If they feel like they are about to be caught and they must tell the truth, they will play the sympathy card to get your mind off of the truth. Later, as you start thinking about what they said, your growing suspicion will impel you to ask questions to find out the truth. They will avoid you and even lie to you to keep their lies from being exposed. Never try to fight with a liar. They have that name for a reason. They will lie and do whatever is necessary so that they do not lose face in front of others.

Unless you are willing to get dirty and beat them at their own game, just stay away from them and cut all ties.

16. Truth Teller—This man believes in being truthful with people. He is a man that rarely lies. He believes that the truth will always come out in the end, so why lie? That is not to say that he has never told a lie in his life. But when I say that he rarely lies, I mean exactly that.

   What to look out for: When you ask this man for the truth, do not expect him to give anything less than that. If you ask him whether you're fat, be prepared for a truthful answer. He will not hurt you just to hurt you. But he believes that the truth is always better than a lie. He is often very blunt in his words, and his tone may often come across as harsh. He is not trying to be hurtful; rather, he just may not have a lot of tact in telling the truth to people. So while he may tell the truth, do not be surprised if what he says hurts. You may have to work with him on how to tell the truth in a way that is not so sharp or biting. Be prepared to put in hours because he will think that you are trying to get him to lie to people. You may have a lot of arguments over what is a lie and how to avoid hurting people's feelings when telling the truth.

17. Scared Man—This man will be afraid to kill a spider. He will not get into a fight for you. If he is held up at gunpoint, then he will run and leave you behind. He may even be scared of germs and different types of insects.

   What to look out for: This type of man will need a very tough woman to compensate for his lack of bravery. This relationship can work just as long as the woman is the opposite of his personality; that way, they both balance each other out. There is someone out there for everyone but it is a matter of finding the right match of personalities so that you can strengthen each other in the areas the other may be weak in.

18. Honorable Man—This man will never run away from a
    fight. There can be thirty guys about to gang up on him
    and he will not back down. He stands up for people who
    can't stand up for themselves. This man is different from
    the *confrontational man*. The difference is in the reason
    each one fights. The confrontational man fights because
    he wants to win arguments. He cannot let anyone win the
    fight. It is more about control and pride than anything
    else. The honorable man fights because he feels that it is
    his duty. He feels that he has to protect the ones he loves
    and those who are not able to fight for themselves.

    What to look out for: This man will always put himself
    in danger's way to prove something to himself, others, and
    his country. He will fight with honor and character, but he
    may leave you behind to do it. Usually these men go into
    the army or the reserves. They may even get caught up in
    gangs because of loyalty and brotherhood. Although this
    man may never cheat on you for another woman, he will
    always be searching for ways to prove his honor and fight
    for his country.

19. Cocky Man—This man believes that he is God's gift to
    women. He believes that women should bow down to
    him. He is not really a picky man. The difference between
    the two is the picky man believes no woman is ever good
    enough for him. He is constantly searching for the right
    one and may not date a woman if she does not meet his
    standards. The cocky man believes that he is just too good
    to be with just one woman. He will even date women that
    the picky man will not. The cocky man is into his looks
    and being adored by many women. He believes a man like
    himself should not be pinned down by just one woman.

    What to look out for: The cocky man does not know
    how to treat a woman because it is all about him. He may
    even fall in love with a woman because she worships the

ground he walks on. That is not love or even a sign of a healthy relationship. To be with this man, you will have to worship and adore him. And even then he will never be in love with you because he is too in love with himself. He may even date and stay in relationships with women who he feels compliments his looks or who can give him even more status.

20. Low Self-Esteem—This man does not believe in himself. He hates his job, his looks, and his life. When you are with him, he will always make you feel like he has the worst luck in the world. He is not trying to manipulate you; he just does not have any confidence in himself.

What to look out for: Trying to actually build up his confidence may actually take yours down. These men seem to be very negative and depressed. If you're an emotional woman, then be very careful in trying to help this man because you may end up depressed. Suggest therapy to this man and see if he is willing to talk to someone. You can be there for him but limit your time with him. That does not mean that you are not a good person because you could not listen to hours and hours of negativity. Just ask yourself this: what kind of friend would be able to help another if they became depressed too? So help him, but sometimes you have to ask them to take the first step on their own.

21. Cheap Man—This man is extremely cheap. Before he even spends a dollar, he has to think about if it is a good idea to spend it. He is not a bad person. He just does not want to pay for anything. If the man has to spend any money in the beginning of the relationship, he will resent you for it. He will be in a bad mood any time he has to spend some money. There will be times when he will spend a little money, but it will be rare.

What to look out for: Most men that are cheap are in debt or have just gotten out of debt. Sometimes men may take on traits that are in their family also. Maybe their dads were cheap, and they have taken on this trait from them. Whatever the reason may be, this man will need someone very understanding. Most women are not gold diggers, but they want to feel appreciated. He will either need to date someone that has similar ideas on money management or someone who can teach him how to spend, but wisely. This man will manage his money well, but he will not like to go out on dates unless you pay for them, or he finds a good deal that he is comfortable paying for.

22. Spending Man—This man does not mind spending a lot of money. He hates penny- pinching his money. He would rather spend all of his money and enjoy the night than try to make his dollars last and not have any fun. This man believes in spoiling himself and the woman he dates with lavish things, whether he can afford them or not. This man will take you to the finest restaurants and will look down at anything cheap. He probably lives in a nice house or a fancy apartment with exotic art.

What to look out for: This man does not know how to manage his money. Even if he can afford it right now, his expensive lifestyle will catch up to him. He tends to spend more than he makes or saves. Short-term relationships will be an experience for you with this man, but do not get into anything long term. You may begin to find yourself spending money after being around him and paying for things that you know are over your budget. Be very careful in a relationship with this man. Be sure to save some money. You never know when it may rain.

23. Player Man—The player's main objective is to add another pair of panties to his collection. The player feels like there is no woman that he cannot talk to. The player's objective

is not to hurt women. His main objective with women is to prove to himself and others that he is smooth. He wants to prove that he has game and that there is no woman he cannot obtain. He will not hurt you or mistreat you physically, but he may hurt your heart if you happen to fall in love with him.

What to look out for: This man is not trying to give his heart to any woman. Players have given their heart to a woman that broke it. There were at least one or two women they fell for without realizing it. But ever since then, they will not let another woman in. They talk to many women for the experience of making love to them rather than being in love with them.

24. Pleaser Man—The pleaser man is different from the *player man*. The pleaser man will go to the ends of the earth to please one woman. He believes that his woman should have all of the finer things in life. He will always give you gifts. You do not have to pay for anything in the relationship. He believes in making his woman happy and he actually finds satisfaction in doing this for his woman.

What to look out for: It is not hard for other women to take advantage of this man too. He easily falls for women that have a tendency to use him. Since he is always trying to please people, it is hard for him to say no to people. Be careful of other women that may try to use him while he is with you. This type of man will buy women things and not demand any sex in return although he may really want to have sex with them. Because of his giving nature, many women may use him unless he finds someone that will love him with or without his gifts.

25. Hypocritical Man—This man is very judgmental. He judges people for things that he does himself. Never try to get encouragement from this man because he has nothing to offer you but judgment. He has a very cruel spirit

and believes in getting ahead even if he has to sacrifice his friends.

What to look out for: This man may actually act like he is not a judgmental person to gain your trust. Once you reveal anything to him, he quickly judges you and may not return your phone calls.

26. Humble Man—He is thankful for everything that he has. He takes pride in working for what he has. It does not matter what he has; he is thankful for everything. He believes in treating people with respect and believes in the good of the world.

What to look out for: You really do not have to look out for anything with this man. One of his flaws is that he trusts people too much. He does not see their true intentions and will be friends with people that mean him no good. He gets hurt a lot when he does find people out for who they truly are. He may experience periods of depression, but other than that this type of man is a god guy.

27. Complaining Man—This guy always feels like he is the victim. Nothing is ever good enough for him. He is always in search of something better than what he has. Although this man complains that people are always taking advantage of him, it is actually the other way around. He plays the victim to evoke sympathy from other to get what he wants.

What to look out for: This man is ruthless in his heart. He will say and do anything to get what he wants out of life. He mainly feeds on women because he knows that women have a gentle heart and love to help anyone in need. Men tend to be too analytical to be fooled and often keep asking questions until they find out what the guy's intentions are. This man knows that all he has to do is appeal to women's emotions and talk about anything sad and he has her. Be very careful of this man because he is good at what he does, and he does not mind using any tactic to get what he wants.

28. Smart Mouth—This guy loves to hear himself talk. It doesn't have to make sense to you as long as it makes sense to him. He always has an opinion about everything. He wants you to agree with him about everything. If you do not agree with him, then he thinks that you are either wrong or stupid. He needs a woman that does not have any strong opinions and does not mind worshipping his "great" mind.

What to look out for: A man that cannot listen to others does not actually respect other people. He thinks of himself as the only one that can be right. And this kind of mentality opens up a world where he will never learn anything new because he thinks that he knows it all.

29. Smart Man—This guy enjoys intellectual debates. He does not try to show off how smart he is but instead prefers to silently show that he is smart by making or designing things. He is often caught reading books or reciting quotes from his favorite author. The man could be on *Jeopardy* because he knows every answer. When you ask him why he doesn't let people know how smart he is, he will just smile at you. Unlike the *Smart Mouth*, this guy does not have to outtalk you in order to show his intelligence.

What to look out for: This man enjoys intellectual stimulation so he really wants to be around someone that can challenge his mind. I'm not saying that you have to recite quotes and carry a book around. All I'm saying is he likes to experience something new and exciting. He likes to have fun by learning new things. Go to the park or a museum. Visit different places and maybe go to different lectures with him. Don't change your personality. If he is going to accept you, then he will accept you for you. But be willing to embrace some of the things that he likes and in return he should embrace some of the things you like. You don't have to talk about sex with this guy to keep his interest. Just be yourself and make an effort to get to know him and the things that he likes.

30. Manipulative Man—This is the guy that looks for your weaknesses and plays on them. If you have fights, he will always go into your past and your childhood and play psychiatrist with your emotions. His main objective is to keep you emotional and confused. This man only thinks of himself. His objective is not to necessarily hurt you but to help himself. This man will not care about you if he cannot use you. Once he can no longer use you, he will throw you away until he needs you again.

What to look out for: This is the type of man that believes in pure loyalty. He does not want you to hurt him, talk about him, or deceive him. He wants you to always be there for him no matter what. He may want you to be around him 24/7 so that he can be sure that you do not stray from being loyal to him. If your family does not like him, he will expect you to choose him over your family. He will give you reasons why he is the victim and they are against him. This man is very charming and will know how to get into your head to keep you feeling like you are confused and lost without him. The extremities of this man are influenced by his experiences, upbringing, emotional stability, and his personality.

31. Romantic Man—This guy will always make you feel as if you are special to him. He always says the right things. He is very romantic and thoughtful. His actions are sincere and he is the type of guy that you end up being high school sweethearts with. He likes romantic walks in the parks and he likes to spend time with the woman that he really cares about.

What to look out for: There is nothing to really look out for with this guy. He is sweet and romantic and he likes to talk for hours. So be prepared to talk because that is very important to him. His first need in the relationship is communication. If he feels that he cannot communicate with his woman, then it is hard for him to feel a connection with you.

32. Bad Boy—This man believes in adventure and just having fun. His agenda in life is to never let anyone tame him. He does what he wants when he wants. One thing about the bad boy is he never lies to women. He tells them the truth and lets them make a choice for themselves what they want to do. He tells them right off that he is not trying to fall in love and this turns on women even more. They want to be the ones that tamed the wild stallion so they set on a mission to tame this wild horse.

What to look out for: Do not try to tame this man because he cannot be captured unless he wants to. You may have caught his body but his mind and heart will always be absent unless he wants to give himself away to a woman.

33. Good Man a.k.a. Mama's Boy—The name pretty much explains itself. He is the opposite of the bad boy and likes to have clean fun. These types of men are looking for a good woman to settle down with. They were raised in a home where marriage was valued. Most of them want to get married, find a good woman, and raise a family with her. They have strong morals and family values. These men are goal oriented and they are all about unity and family.

What you should look out for: Do not talk bad about his mama. He respects his mama and he wants his girlfriend or future wife to get along well with her. Most of the time, the moms of these types of men sabotage their sons' relationships because they don't think there are women that can ever be good enough for them. So the mom and the girlfriend always have to struggle to get along. If you can get off on the right foot with his mom, then you have already won this man's heart.

34. The Addict—This man always has something that he is addicted to. It can be pills, drugs, hot sauce, sex, flirting, abusiveness, gambling, drinking, etc. These men may be very superstitious and believe in quick rich schemes. It's like they have no direction in life and are a leaf in the wind. Everything seems to influence their behavior. If they had a bad day, they want their addiction. If they are happy, they want their addiction. If they think about something from their past, they want their addiction. If you try to talk to them about stopping their addiction, they want it even more. It may even get to the point that they begin to stop functioning in the world for weeks or months if they cannot get to their addiction.

What to look out for: Basically if you keep seeing continuous patterns in his behavior that do not change, then let this man go. If his behavior towards you and others is very negative when he does these things, then let this man go. Do not think how you can help him beyond giving him information on where to go to get help. Many women have become addicted as well trying to save these men. The man might have been addicted to sex and then the woman becomes addicted to sex. The guy might have been addicted to drinking and months later it comes out that the woman is going to AA meetings to try to get over her drinking problem. We all want to help people but if they do not want to change or help themselves, then any suggestions are just a form of nagging to them. First you have to believe that you have a problem before you allow someone to help you. If these men do not believe that they have a problem, then they will think they do not need help.

35. The Simple Man—This man will not even take medicine when he has a headache. He does not drink alcohol, and he does not do any illegal drugs. Before he takes anything, he has to have a doctor's prescription. He does not like to follow the crowd, and he likes to be in control of his behavior. He does not read a lot of books because he thinks that people just try to control you with their opinions through them. This man will not eat a lot of candy because it has too much sugar in it. He does not watch a lot of TV because he says it has too much violence and crime on it. This man is the type that hates to feel like someone is controlling him or making him go along with society. He is not a rebel or radical man. He is just a simple man that wants to live a simple life. He is more about being self-sufficient than relying on society to give him quick fixes. If something does not feel right with him, then he does not do it. He doesn't want to live in the times before there were no toilets, but he doesn't want to feel like society is controlling what he does or what he says either. He pays his taxes and he follows guidelines, but he is a leader and not a follower.

What to look out for: Just be yourself around this guy. Do not try to get him to loosen up and take a drink or get wild because he will quickly cut you off. He does not try to control others and what they do and he asks for the same respect. Just know that if you are looking to drink, go to a wild party, and let loose, then he is not going. But if you are looking for a quiet evening or you want to go to a movie, this is your guy.

These are just a few of the personality traits of men that you may encounter in your lifetime. Do not be afraid to meet men;

they cannot hurt you unless you let the wrong man into your heart. Don't be afraid to talk to people or live life, but be on the lookout for the warning signs that give you clues into a man's personality that he is not the right one for you. It's all about compatibility. If you know that you do not like anyone telling you what to do, then stay clear of a controlling man. If you do not like it when men flirt with other women, then stay clear of men that cannot control their need to flirt.

Never try to change a man. If he does not want to change, you will always have ups and downs in the relationship trying to come to some agreement on how to make things better. Some things are a work in progress like becoming more organized, learning not to worry about things, being less clingy, or becoming more independent. But some men will have issues like drug, sex, hitting, flirting, playing games, manipulation, and addictions. They have been like this for years, and just because you decide that it is not a good idea for them to be like this anymore does not mean that they are going to change for you.

If you feel like you have the strength mentally and physically to deal with it, then it will be a long journey to recovery. Sometimes they may do well for weeks and maybe months and then have a relapse. You have to go through the journey of ups and downs with them and just be prepared for anything you get into or stay in. I'm not saying there won't be times when the guy really wants to change. But he has to want to change first. You cannot suggest the idea and think that he will.

I will say that it will be easier for you to get a guy that is compatible with your personality. We meet men all the time that have charm and game but they are the wrong ones for us. Being with these men means sacrificing your health, happiness, and even maybe your money. In other words, they are like leeches; they take more than they give and they still need more even if you are drained.

Do not allow yourself to get to know these men when you see the signs. It's harder to let go after you start to like the guy and have had sex with him. But it's not hard to let go in the first stages of dating. Dating is a process—a process that allows us to date until we find the right one that we are compatible with. So when you see the signs that this man is not compatible with you and means you no good, then leave him. A lot of times, you will not be able to tell right off, but there will be signs that alert you that something is wrong.

DON'T BECOME THE STATISTIC

Keep your eyes open in any relationship so that you can see the warning signs. No matter what anyone tells you, there are always warning signs in relationships. You can choose to ignore them, or you can use them to detour you from getting hurt in a relationship. Once you become hurt, it is easy to throw away good men.

Warning signs alert you to the fact that someone may not be right for you. They are there to protect your mind, body, and heart from a very bad relationship. Do not feel guilty for having these feelings. If something is not right in your heart about a person, then that feeling is there for a reason. It's there to help protect you.

For example, if your boyfriend never calls you, then he may be in another relationship. Sometimes really "doggish" men will lead you on knowing they are with someone. If he cheats on you in the very beginning of the relationship, then do not overlook this. If he is cheating and looking at every woman that you pass, then do not have sex with this man. Do not become his girlfriend. Do not go and get married to him. End the relationship immediately.

If you are with a man that gets upset very easily, then precede with caution. Watch for signs that he may be abusive by seeing how the women in his life respond to him. Does he treat his mom with respect and love? Does his mom look at you with desperation in her eyes like you need to run? Do his sisters or friends hint to you that he was involved in some domestic abuse situations in the past? I won't say that sometimes people don't lie about other people. But when people tell you things and you see the signs, then please do not ignore the situation.

If a guy talks about how he is a good and religious person, but he sends you nasty pictures and talks about sex all the time, run from him. This guy is a hypocrite and is playing a game with you to get what he wants. If you are talking to a guy on the phone and he keeps telling you to hold on to answer another call, then nine times out of ten, it may be his girlfriend or his wife. He may try to say that it is just a friend or his mother calling on the other line but keep in mind that you do not really know the guy to believe that. So do not rule out the fact that it can in fact be another woman or his girlfriend.

It is important to look for a man that knows the value of a dollar. This isn't to say that he can never buy anything for himself, but he must also know how to save. If a guy spends a lot of money in the relationship on watches and clothes, then think twice before being with this guy. He is a big spender and may not know how to budget his money. If you look at a man who has a lot of watches, rings, necklaces, suits, designer clothes, and shoes but he has a big dent in his car, then think about being with him. He does not know how to prioritize his money. He has spent all of his money on his appearances so he doesn't have any money left to fix the dent in his car. This tells you that his priorities are more on being flashy and impressing people than paying his bills. That means that all of his money is on his back and not in his pockets or the bank. So it is pretty safe to say that if he cannot manage his own money, then he will start asking you for some. You will spend a lot of money on this man to help him pay bills while he saves his for his own personal use.

I'm not saying that the man has to have a large bank account. What I am saying is you want to know that your man has the ability to plan for the future. Maybe one day you might want to get married, have children, or buy a house. It is important that you both know how to budget your money for bills or unexpected emergencies that might come up. If he spends all of his money frivolously now, then that tells you where his priorities will be down the road. Little signs like these may save you a lot of heartache later.

WHEN MARRIAGE HAPPENS

Another thing to look at when you are in a relationship with a man is how long it takes him to know that he really wants to be with you. Of course no one is going to get married on the first date. That would be unrealistic. When a man really cares for you, then it doesn't take him ten years to know if he wants to marry you or not. If it takes a man that long, then he doesn't plan on marrying you. Different circumstances may cause a man to delay marrying you such as school, army, or a death in the family. That is understandable for him to ask you to wait until a appropriate time, which will not cause stress on you both.

The depression comes when women who have been with their man for over seven years see other women getting married after two years and they are still not married. The guys these women are with may not ever plan to marry. They like their situation just the way it is. To them, they like being committed in a relationship without really being legally tied to anyone, as anytime he wants to leave, he can. There is no commitment to you or to God that he wants to be with you for better or for worse. If you really want to get married and this man makes you wait a decade, then he is stalling. Of course, you don't want to get married to anyone without being sure that this person is the right one. For every couple, the exact time when they'll be ready is going to be different. But if it has been over five years and he still has not shown any desire to marry you, then he plans to keep things the way they are.

Marriage is not a deed saying that you own the other person. It is a bond between two people that signifies that they have become one in mind, body, heart, and soul. After five years have passed, and he is still trying to make the excuse that he needs more time, then you may want to evaluate the relationship. Don't wait until you become so depressed that you give up on love. Act before you get to the depression stage, so you can be with someone else with the same marriage goals as you. Men know in the first two years of dating you if they want to marry you or not. Most men that want to get married go ahead and do so in the first three years of their relationship. There are cases though where it may take a couple a little longer to know if they actually are the right ones for each other. But basically, it does not take a man half of his lifetime to know if he wants to be with you or not.

SHOULD I GIVE HIM THE ULTIMATUM?

That is a good question. The ultimatum is often used in relationships when the woman feels like the man is having his cake and eating it too. A lot of times when women give men the ultimatum, it causes problems in the relationship. He has to make the choice to marry you or you are moving on with someone else. In most cases, the ultimatum is more for the woman than it is for the man. She needs to know where the relationship is going before she gives any more of herself to it. Sometimes a man will get confused. He may really want to marry a woman, but he just isn't quite sure that he really wants to give up the single life. Give him a little time because you want it to be his choice. You do not want to make it seem as if you are pushing him into doing what you want. We discussed earlier that the human will is too strong and you cannot force any one to do what he does not want to do. When he makes the decision for himself, he will know he married you because that is what he wanted to do in his heart. When he feels that you have pushed him into the marriage through nagging and threats, then he'd feel he was forced. If he feels forced, then in the back of his mind, he may doubt if he really is ready or if you are really the one.

Do not take that to mean that you have to stay in the relationship without voicing how you feel. Tell the man how you feel and then move on. Women have to reflect whether they want to leave or stay in the relationship as well. They have to figure out if the relationship is going somewhere or if they are better off moving on. Do not try to change a man that does not want to be tied down. Instead, find a man that actually wants to get married one day. You deserve that. There are still men out there that want to be with someone that they can talk to and spend time with. It is hard to leave any relationship in which you have invested time, energy, and emotions. That is why both the man and the woman have to sit down and have a long talk. They both have to decide whether they can or cannot live without each other.

THE FRIEND THEORY

Do not let a man sleep with you but yet only call you his friend or his friend with benefits. Please know his behavior is saying, "I don't want to have a relationship. I really just want the intimacy." Some men feel that women give up intimacy more freely when they feel they are in a relationship or some sort of a beginning to it. This tactic is used to string women along to believe that they are in a relationship when they are not. It's more like the guy is getting his cake and eating it too. The woman is led to believe that they are taking the relationship slow but they are just not using titles. She believes that they will eventually use them, but right now they are just taking things slow. In most cases the man is really getting one over her because he has no plans of taking the relationship to the next level.

Some men will even try to convince you that the lack of labels such as *girlfriend* or *boyfriend* does not mean anything. "It's just a title; we're really dating." In the same situation with a woman he really cared about, she would have a title, especially if he was around his friends and they were looking at her. I bet he'd be quick to say then that she is his girlfriend.

THINK ABOUT IT THIS WAY

What if you are dating a guy who calls you his friend and you get intimate with each other? You spend time together and you go out on dates every week. If you see him with another girl, can you get upset if you are supposedly just "friends"? The fact that you got upset lets you know that in your mind you are not just friends. If you get upset at the thought of him being with somebody else, then he is not just your friend. People who are just friends date other people.

So you're upset and you decide to go up to the girl that he is with. You stare each other down and you ask the question: "Who are you?" She replies, "Who are you?" "I'm his friend," you respond. She says, "I'm his girlfriend."

Titles mean a lot in society. This is what distinguishes one person from the next. You would not call a child "Mister." You would not call a man a boy. You would not call a woman a girl. You would not call a lawyer a doctor. You would not call a husband a boyfriend or a wife a friend. Titles do have importance and significance.

- What if a man said he was a lawyer but he was going to perform surgery without a medical license?

- What if a policeman said he would perform your root canal but he was not a dentist?

- What if a man chased you down for speeding but said he was just a dentist?

- What if a couple were married but told everybody they were just friends?

Not only does the lack of labels give other people mixed signals but it confuses the man and the woman. Both people should be on the same page. One person should not believe they are in a relationship while the other person believes that they are only friends. That causes a lot of pain and grief. Always discuss the terms of the relationship so that you can make sure you both are in sync. You don't have to ask every week but at some point discuss where the relationship is going.

LIVING TOGETHER: ROMANCE AND EVERYTHING ELSE

A lot of people are living together today and are finding out that they have dated a totally different person from the one that they met when they were still dating. Be very careful before you move in with a man. You might find out that you do not know him as well as you think. It's so romantic when you first start dating and you go to your place and he goes to his. But when you live together, that arrangement can change your mind about the other person and you begin to see what married life would be like without actually having a ring.

A woman may want the ring after a certain amount of time but the man is not yet ready. When you live together with a man before you get married, you set him up to feel comfortable living with you without actually committing to you. In other words, when you feel like you have lived together long enough and you would like to get married, your man may prefer to keep things as they are. He may feel like things are going fine. Why change it by moving too fast into marriage? The woman may feel like they are already married and doing things that married people do. Why not go ahead and get married? That is when the conflict comes in. He feels like things are going fine. He has already proven that he wants to commit to her by moving in and saying she is the only one that he wants to be with. Why rush to get married and mess up anything when technically he has already given his loyalty without the ring or the paper? He may feel like you didn't want a ring when you moved in so why should he give you one now?

Once a man feels comfortable with how things have been, he may not want to change. That is why how you start off with a man is so important. If you want him to marry you, then let him know after a reasonable amount of time that you're looking for a commitment and not just a good time. Don't scare him on the first date talking about marriage too early. There's nothing wrong with knowing what you want but you both have just met. So he does not even know if this is going to work out. And think about how you would feel if you did not really know a guy and already he was asking for sex. You would think to yourself, *I don't even know this man. He hasn't even paid for the meal, we haven't even talked for ten minutes, and he has the audacity to try to get in my pants.*

Just because you live with a man doesn't mean he will not want to marry you. Likewise, just because someone does not live with a man doesn't mean he will want to marry them. The main point I'm trying to make is that when you live with a man there is a lot more to it than romantic nights and cuddling. So before you move in with a man, be aware that you may be getting the married life without necessarily getting the ring.

When the relationship ends, who gets the apartment? When you're in a relationship or in love with someone, the last thing on your mind is splitting up. But if it happens, who stays and who leaves? What happens in a lot of relationships is that the man and the woman find out that they are incompatible. They may even find themselves arguing over everything. Maybe the guy cheated and the woman leaves. Maybe it's the other way around: the girl cheated and the guy kicked her out. Whatever the reason, they may be stressed out trying to find other living arrangements once the relationship is over. Some people stay friends and may decide to keep living with each other. They may see other people, but it may be very awkward to see someone else kissing and hugging your ex. Then, it may also depend on how close they were to each other; the apartment may evoke too many bad memories, and in this case, staying would not be an option. How two people split up would depend on the persons involved, the relationship, and how things happened. But there is an old saying that says, "Don't put all of your eggs in one basket"; this means that you should always think towards the future when making present decisions. You may be living with this guy now but what happens when the relationship goes south? What would be your back-up plan for living arrangements? Always have a back-up plan just in case things do not work out.

There are also differences in living styles. We all know that everyone has a certain way of doing things. So if he is very messy and you are very clean, that is going to be a cause for conflict right there. That's not to say that it would be impossible for the both of you to get used to each other. It's just that it will take a lot of will power and adjustment.

Another thing that may not be so good about living together is that sometimes things change unexpectedly. Say you are splitting the rent and you both pay half, but then he loses his job and now all of the responsibility is on you. It didn't start out that way, but life happened and you have to work two jobs just to come up with the rent. Or maybe he still has his job, but something came up and he had to use the money for the rent. He promises to pay you back but something always comes up. So now you not only have to deal with a relationship, you have to deal with the finances too. A lot of times, the stress of handling the finances will break up the couple or cause great tension between them. So be aware that things do change before you decide to live with each other. There are some good men out there that do not use women and pay their own bills. But no one is immune from life and the unexpected changes that it will bring.

There is also the time and space a couple gives to each other. This is very important before you decide to live with someone. When you first meet someone, you don't mind spending time with them because it is new and exciting. Then after the romance dies down and you start getting to know one another, spending time together may not seem as exciting as before. You may notice more silences or misunderstandings than before. When you're dating and living in separate places, you may feel like you want to see the other person more because you both have your space and time to be alone. When you live together, then you make a commitment that your space is his space and his space is your space. So just adjusting to his routine and yours will be something that will take compromise. Maybe he has set a night to be his time to play cards with his buddies and smoke cigars. You don't smoke and you come home wanting peace and quiet only to find that the TV is blasting and there is smoke filling in the room and the place looks a mess.

Remember this is what he's been doing before you came into his life but now that you are living together, he may still want to do the things he did before. On your part, maybe you like going to the club with your friends for a girls' night out and he feels that since you are in a relationship, you should stay home more and clean up. So be very sure once you have decided to live with each other that you have laid the ground rules and thought everything out very carefully. If you are reading this book, then you are old and mature enough to make your own decisions and choices. I'm not telling you not to live with a man if it is your choice to do so, but look at all the pros and cons before you make that move.

LONG DISTANCE RELATIONSHIPS: NEED GLUE?

One of the issues of many relationships is the viability of long distance relationships. How do you keep a long distance relationship together when you may not be able to see the other person as much as you would like? I'm not going to tell you that these relationships never work because that would be unrealistic. But I will say that they are very hard because the distance and physical absence takes a toll on both people. For a long distance relationship to succeed, it will require work from both people and not just one. You should not feel that you are doing all the work in the relationship. If you go to see him one weekend, then he should see you the next. When one person feels like they are doing all the work in the relationship, then that is when problems start to arise.

Long distance relationships require a lot of communication because each person cannot see the other person like they would like to. One thing that would help is if both split the responsibility of traveling to see one another. If the man travels all the time, then he gets tired and eventually stops coming to see the woman because of money and gas. If the woman travels all the time, then she feels like she is doing all the work and the man is not taking any responsibility. So agreeing on times and days on when they will each see each other will save the other person from feeling that they are the only ones doing all the work.

Designate a time when both of you can talk on the phone about your day and discuss different topics. The topics don't have to be planned, but you should both be open to how the other person feels and what they would like to talk about. One thing that I do know about long distance relationships is communication is the number one priority. Since you cannot physically see the person as much as you would like, it is important to be able to communicate verbally.

I'm not trying to scare any woman but I'm just trying to give them the whole scope on long distance relationships. Nine times out of ten, men stay faithful for about a month or two. He doesn't talk or see other women beyond the friendship stage. He is not having sex with a woman, except for you when you do make visits to him. He comes down every weekend and he seems like he is really happy to see you and he is there physically and mentally. Then he skips a couple of weekends because he says that he has to work or there is some activity going on that week that he does not want to miss (birthday party, basketball game, tournament, child's birthday, or he is spending time with the kids). You feel disappointed but believe him because this is the first time that he missed in months. You may only get to see each other on weekends so you understand that he may need a day from the weekend to do what he needs to do since he is working the rest of the week. But after that, you notice he is starting to make more and more excuses not to see you. He does not want to talk on the phone as much anymore. When you try to call him, he does not return your call until much later or the next day. He is tired from work and you really start to think at first that he is lonely and may miss you. So you decide to take some vacation time off of work and go spend a week or several days with him.

WHEN HE LETS YOU COME OVER, IT IS NOT THE SAME.

He is distant, he acts like he does not want to have sex anymore, and he feels obligated to spend time with you. He keeps his phone near him and checks it often. He is cold and short with you and all he wants to do is eat or sleep. If you ask him if anything is wrong, he will say he is just tired and will probably say that his head is hurting. You get upset because you took that time off and you feel like it was a waste of time. If you suggest that next time he takes some time off to see you, he will say that he will see, that he has been working a lot of hours lately and he does not know if the boss will let him take time off. Then it will come out later that he took some time off during the week to go see his kids or just to relax. You will wonder why he did not tell you and he will say that he really needed some time to just relax and de-stress. He would have told you, but he knows that you had to work and had a lot going on, and he did not want to bother you. If you ask him to take some more time off and spend it with you, he will say that he just took some off.

HE DOESN'T LET YOU COME TO SPEND TIME WITH HIM, AND THEN DOESN'T CALL YOU AS MUCH WHILE YOU ARE OFF.

If you call him, he will make an excuse why he will be busy for the next couple of hours. He may even say he was called into work or he had to spend more time at work to get a project done. The next time he comes to see you, he is in a very bad mood. He says that he just has a lot on his mind, and he may not be able to do this every weekend anymore because his shifts changed at work, he has the kids, he's getting tired of traveling down here (it's too expensive), and he misses you too much and does not get to see you and that is hard on him.

Most men after this will stop calling you or they will officially break it off over the phone, in an e-mail, or in a text message. You are heartbroken because you knew he was distant and unhappy, but he blamed it on so many things. You start replaying everything in your mind to see why he cut things off just like that without talking to you. It may be that he was spending time with another woman all the while and he did not cut it off until he felt that he was closer to the other woman. So that is why he gave you just enough to keep you in the relationship. Now that he and the other woman are closer, he decides that it is better to cut things off with you. He may have felt guilty for leading you on and just wanted to end things so that you did not get hurt. You are even more hurt because he should have told you this sooner instead of stringing you along.

That is not to say that most men will break it off with you. Some of the more trifling ones will have sex with you and another woman that they spend most of their time with when you are not around. They do not plan on leaving you at all, but they do need more sex than what you are giving them on the weekend. To them, it may not even be cheating because they are only looking at it as a need that is being taken care of. They do not love the other woman, but they do have needs. If you ever decide to move to where he is, then he may cut it off depending on the depth of attachment that he has with her. Whether she wants to cut it off is another story. It depends on what he told her. Most men will say that they had a girlfriend, but they cut it off as soon as they moved to a new city. Some will say that they do have a girlfriend, but that they are having problems with them. A few may actually say they have one but they have needs that aren't taken care of. Only a few are actually this honest with the other woman. The majority of men may not even tell her about you at all. She is kind of like you. She thinks that she is his girlfriend, and she may have suspicions that he is cheating with another woman. She does not know that she was the other woman and that he is cheating on you with her.

YOU DECIDE TO MOVE SO THAT YOU ARE CLOSER TO HIM.

Be very careful. Make sure it is love before you do that. Know the kind of man that you have and what his character is. I have seen too many situations where the woman moved, and then they broke up two months after she moved to be with the man. They were supposed to move in together but she ended up having to get her own place, or she did move in but had to get her own place after they broke up. I'm not going to even go into detail about the pain and financial burden this wrong move puts women in. They had suspicions that he might be seeing someone or things were distant between them, but they thought the move would make things better because the guy could see them more.

Allow the guy to move to where you are because that shows you that he actually wants to be with you. Never move yourself because he might have moved on in the relationship; he is just not telling you. Or sometimes, men can be unsure about what they want to do and who they actually want. It does not take them a whole year to make up their mind. This debating process lasts no longer than two weeks. During this period, they weigh all the pros and cons of your relationship—how long you have been together, how he feels when he is with you, whether you have been there for him, whether you can take care of him (sexually, financially, and emotionally), whether he can live without you, and whether he plans to marry you one day. He then does the same thing with the other woman. After he has made his decision, he does not tell you right away. He is thinking about the best way to break the news to you. It always comes out in behavior what a person is thinking about and how a person feels toward you. For men, they are not good at really talking to women about their feelings so it comes out a lot in their behavior. Your man gets shorter in his conversations with you. He gets upset easily and he may even point out all of your faults. He does not want to talk to you or even see you anymore. He just really hopes that you get the hint so that he does not seem like the bad guy.

The difference between women and men is the way they are allowed to express their emotions. Men feel emotions just like women, but they express theirs differently than women do. They will not cry in front of you and they will not fall to the fall and beg you not to go. They may do it later if they feel that is the last resort, but it won't happen in the beginning. They may even try to give you a logical reason why you should stay and why you should not go, but other than that, they let their emotions come out through their behavior. They may start drinking and partying more, and they may become more sexually active and physically aggressive. They actually divert their emotions into behavior.

Women tend to express their emotions more. We talk, yell, scream, cuss, and argue out our emotions. A man may clam up and just not want to talk anymore and he will go out and express what he is feeling through his behavior. So that is one of the reasons why women will never hear the guy really come out and say, "Hey, I want to break up." Trust me when I say he will show you long before he says it, if he ever really says it. Some men will actually say the words, "I want to break up." But this is not how the majority of men act.

The only way for you to truly know what is going on and what a man wants to do is to come out and say it. Don't beat around the bush; just ask him if he is cheating on you and if he has any plans for the relationship. Most men will be real with you. They will let you know if they are just having fun, if they think you are good as a girlfriend but not a wife, or if they cannot live without you. Men tend to be honest when it comes to the status of the relationship. But if you turn around and ask them if they are cheating, they may start an argument by saying that they are not cheating and that you are only paranoid. Do not do this unless you are for real and really want to break up. But one of the ways to know if a man wants to break up with you is how fast he says it is over too. You know the times when you want to break up and the guy begs you and he calls and tries to make up? Well, that is a guy that does not want to leave. Do you remember the times when you say you want to break up and the guy says, "If that is what you want to do, then fine!" And then it may take him a week or two to call? Well that guy was debating if he wanted to stay with you or not. He may have had just a friend he was talking to but they became close. So he may debate if he wants to move on or give it another chance. Well, since he called you back, he decided to give it another chance. But when it takes him too long to call you back, be very careful and keep your options open because he is close to leaving. When the man says fine after you said you wanted to break up, then he was just looking for the opportunity to break up. Some men will even start an argument so that you will get mad and break up with them. They are hoping you will get so mad that you will end it. If he says fine too quick, then that is what he has wanted to do for a while; he just did not want to be the one to actually initiate the break up.

So before you move, be sure that what you have is leading to marriage or at least has a very strong foundation. Relationships are so hard because you give this guy a year or more and it's over. You can feel like he does not want to fight as much for your love as you do. But men feel this way. You are not his wife so he will not be committed to you but there is also more fish in the sea. So that is why a woman has to make sure they are both on the same page before she thinks it is heading to marriage or decides to move in with him.

I'm not telling you to leave or stay. Before you commit to someone, make sure you are both on the same page. Let the guy initiate most of the moves. You know how you feel but you don't know how he feels. Most men don't even tell you when they are starting to date other people until the very end. To see if he is still into you, let him initiate and make most of the moves. If he isn't calling you as much, then don't keep calling him. If he does not want to see you as much, then don't do all the traveling. When you see him pulling back, then you pull back too. That allows you to keep your emotions out of a relationship that will eventually end up at a dead end. If he is making an effort, then by all means make an effort too. But what most women tend to do is give and give, while the guy is giving nothing back.

Most guys like long distance relationships because they really do not have to commit to a woman. All he has to do is call and see her on most weekends. Sometimes he may have to travel to see a woman which is okay, because he gets a vacation and plenty of sex when he wants it. It may even be a break away from the other woman when they have a fight. Long distance relationships can work if both people are willing to make an effort, but you cannot be the only one. One of the most important things to remember in this kind of relationship is to know when to pull away. It may hurt for a while, but if he is not giving back in the relationship then don't carry the load for both people.

GET IT OUT! DON'T EAT IT UP!

Everybody deals with things in their life that they may need to talk about. There is nothing wrong with talking to a therapist about your problems. I often hear some women say,

"I don't need therapy, I need a man," "Sane people do not need a therapist," or "Crazy people see a therapist." Talking to a therapist is not about strength or weakness. Talking to a therapist helps you keep your sanity and deal with issues in a positive manner. Everybody talks to a therapist whether they know it or not. These therapists do not get paid and are on call twenty-four hours a day. They are called friends, brothers, sisters, parents, or mentors. When you are having a bad day, you call your friend. It does not matter if they want to hear about your day. You are going to tell them anyway. Everybody needs to talk to somebody that they trust. Getting out those negative vibes does not mean that you are crazy or weak. It shows that you are healthy and know how to express your emotions in a healthy way.

Are you the kind of person that keeps all your feelings inside? Do you never tell one soul how your day is going? I don't suggest telling everyone your business but find someone that you trust and let it out. The person who is giving you advice should be someone that also takes their own advice. The first and one of the most important steps to healing is being able to talk about your feelings. Do not keep your feelings trapped inside. In any healthy relationship, both people will have to learn how to talk about their feelings and communicate effectively.

Gaining weight is not fun at all. A lot of times, instead of dealing with our problems, we are tempted to just stuff ourselves with food. Society has taught us that a cookie makes everything better. When a child hurts themselves, we offer them sweets to make them feel better. What do you do to cope? When you have a bad day at work, do you reach for vegetables or sweets? After a break up, are you tempted to get into those baggy sweatpants and eat ice cream and cookies in front of the TV? It's easy to feel like eating will make you feel better. But all it does is make you feel guilty for pigging out. Then you have to eat more because eating does not take away the problem. One thing to do when you are dealing with a break up or coping with being single is to stay active. Keep your mind busy. Do not focus on your problems; rather, work on helping others. Do not keep yourself busy to the point that you tie up all your time with work. Overexertion does not keep your mind occupied; all it does is tire you out and make you more miserable. You should balance work and relaxation so that your mind gets its needed rest. Fill up your time with meaningful things like spending time with your family. Work on your hobbies. Give some of your time to organizations or good causes. Do something constructive with your time that causes you to burn calories, not put them on.

When you put on weight, it causes you to be unhappy with everything else in your life. It affects your job and how you feel about yourself. It affects your self-esteem and your standards in relationships. Some men can be jerks, but some women, especially those that are overweight, feel that they have no choice but to accept that behavior.

As a person that has spent my life fluctuating in weight, I identify with the feeling of being overweight and feeling unattractive and unaccepted. There is nothing wrong with women being different sizes and being different. I know in order to be a model you have to be a particular size. I'm not saying that it is not important to eat healthy and exercise. Being healthy and exercising is a great way to relieve stress and take better care of yourself. But even if you are not a size four, you shouldn't become discouraged. The problem only comes when you are not happy with your weight and you keep eating because you are unhappy. Once this happens, you start to accept any relationship that comes along. Or you begin starving yourself to become the size that you think is acceptable to others.

So never accept anything that is not good for you when it comes to relationships. Be realistic in your standards but do not put yourself down and feel like you have to settle because of your weight. I would suggest working on your weight before you date. I did not say lose forty or fifty pounds before dating. When you begin to work on it, you start to feel like you are in control of the situation rather than the other way around. You will be surprised how that affects your self-confidence, and it will show in your relationships. When you feel down about yourself, it's easy to feel defeated and set low goals because you feel like you're asking for too much. There is actually a saying that goes, "It is better to aim high and miss than to aim low and make it." Once you feel good about yourself, it begins to affect every area of your life. Your perception, ideas, and self image influences all areas of your life.

MEN AND WOMEN ARE DIFFERENT

Yes, men act and think differently from women. But they are not complicated. They are human beings just like we are. They feel emotion just as much as women do. The only difference is men are taught to control their emotions. Women are allowed to cry but men are not. Society categorizes men as "weak" if they cry in public. The way men and women express their emotions are different. But the way men and women feel or experience emotions is the same. Everybody has experienced love, pain, hurt, depression, anger, happiness, joy, anxiety, frustration, and sadness at some point in their life. I've never heard a man say that he did not feel these things. He just may not want to talk about it in depth. But men do experience every emotion that a woman does because we are all humans. The way that each sex interprets and displays these emotions is the only thing that is different.

As a woman, it is important that we don't stress ourselves out trying to read men's every move. Men are not written in another language. Listen to your man's words but do not dissect each part. If you are wondering what a man meant by a particular statement then just ask him. If a man's behavior is confusing you then bring it to his attention. If he changes his behavior patterns after you have expressed your concerns then he is listening to you. The way to communicate with a man is just to tell him how you feel in a calm manner. For every action, there is a reaction. If you want to have a calm and effective conversation, do not become defensive when expressing your feelings. Tell him how you feel and wait for him to respond. If you express your feelings in an angry or aggressive manner, he will get offended and express his feelings in the same tone that you expressed yours.

Communication is the key to any relationship whether it is a friendship or a professional relationship. Without communication and understanding on both ends, misunderstandings are sure to arise and never become resolved. Part of what causes a misunderstanding to ruin relationships is when both people don't talk and communicate. We all think and react differently to things. Whenever something is bothering you, do not hold it in. Let the other person know how you feel in a respectful way and talk it out. The other person may not have even known that they did or said anything that bothered you.

THE CELL PHONE RULE

Does a man really have to show a woman his cell phone in order to show the woman that he is not cheating? Not necessarily. If a man really wants to cheat on you, he can cheat without a cell phone. There is certainly nothing wrong with having an open relationship where you and your partner check each other's phones. You may feel you have nothing to hide from each other. There is certainly nothing wrong with that. On the other hand, if a man does not want to show you his phone then that does not mean that he is cheating on you. Believe me there are other ways to find out if a man is cheating on you other than checking his cell phone. You can argue by saying, "If he is not cheating, then why in the world does he not want to show me his cell phone?" The following are some valid reasons:

1. In a relationship, trust should not have to be proven with just a cell phone.

2. He could feel that he shouldn't have to be forced to show you his phone just to prove that he is not cheating.

3. The human will is too strong to make anyone do something that they are not willing to do.

4. Cell phones do not make people cheat. Just because a man has a cell phone does not mean that he is going to cheat if it is not his will to do so.

5. Trust is not found in a phone; it is supposed to be in your man.

6. It is an invasion of privacy. It also indicates a lack of trust and confidence on your part.

7. He could always erase the number, use a fake name, or he can actually have a second phone you know nothing about. The second phone he leaves out could be a decoy to make you feel like he is sharing everything in his life with you.

8. You become obsessed with the suspicion that he could be cheating. You're not able to have a good time with him because you're constantly driving yourself insane about every text and every call he receives. If he is cheating, you do not have to go crazy trying to figure out when, where, and why it happened. Many women have caught their men on dates, in bed, and kissing other women. If he is cheating, it will come to light. But do not drive yourself crazy looking for it.

The list could go on and on. There is nothing wrong with a man showing or not showing his phone to a woman. Try not to jump to conclusions without exclusive evidence. There are too many ways to tell if a man is cheating than just by looking at his cell phone. A woman should be able to tell by the lack of affection in a relationship. You can tell by his patterns if anything has changed. He rarely comes home to you anymore. He doesn't want you to touch him. He makes every excuse as to why he cannot see you. Every time you plan a date, he cancels it. Lately, he starts an argument every time you are with him. He doesn't want to talk as much as he used to. He's talking more to his cell phone than to you. You smell perfume on him. He smells like soap but his job is not indoors. You might find numbers in his pockets or other female products at his place that are not yours. He takes the longest time to answer your texts or your calls. Sometimes you do not hear a reply from him until the next day. And the list goes on and on.

I encourage no woman to go down the list and stress herself out to see if her man is cheating. I am only saying if the signs are there, do not ignore them. Don't try to go find the other woman and confront her. This action does not make the situation better; it will only make the situation worse. Talk to someone you trust before you react. Take some time to calm down and then confront your man about the issue. If nothing can be resolved in a calm manner between you two, then get out of the relationship if it is not working.

WHEN DID THE MOUSE CHASE THE CAT?

When a man wants to get to know you, he will pursue you. Today, it seems as if the roles have reversed and it's the women who pursue the men. This only causes stress and future hurt for the women. A man that cares and wants to get to know a woman will pursue her. If he is not the one that is pursuing you, then any effort on your part will seem like desperation to him. A lot of women get hurt because they have pursued a man who does not care for them. I know it may seem like this rule is old-fashioned and was used in your grandmother's day. Actually, this rule still applies to women today. I'm not saying that it is wrong to start a conversation with a man. I'm not saying that you cannot go out to lunch with a man or be friends. What I'm saying is men will make an effort if they are really interested in a woman.

Some women use the excuse that men today are so shy. If they waited for a man to pursue them, they could be waiting forever. Again, this statement is not true. Yes, some men are shy. Just like some women are shy. What makes the statement untrue is that even though the man is shy, he will still make an effort to speak to you if he is interested. He will call you without you having to initiate all the calls. He will call you to set up dates without you having to ask him.

If you are doing all the calling, then he is not into you and he may be hoping that you stop calling him. If you are paying for all the dates, then he does not care for you. He may be using you just for a free movie or dinner without having to spend his own money. This may sound like I am being very harsh and mean. I am not trying to be mean. I am just telling you the truth. When a man cares for you, then he makes a lot of plans to see you again. Think about it this way. What if you didn't really care for a guy? You went out on a date or two and you're not really feeling him.

Are you going to call him every day and set up more dates? You're probably not going to call him and hope he gets the message after you don't show an interest in him.

On the other hand, if you really care for this guy then you don't mind him calling you or scheduling more dates. When the woman pursues the man, it turns him off because he thinks that she is desperate. In his mind, he thinks that she keeps pursuing him despite his lack of interest in her. There are a few men out there that will come out and tell you that they are not interested in you. Most men are not that way. They will show you through their actions and hope that you get the hint. The best way for a woman to not get hurt is to let the man pursue her. That way, a woman doesn't have to guess if he likes her and look for signs. The fact that he is the one that is pursuing you and contacting you for further dates is a really big plus. I'm not trying to tell any woman to close her eyes in the relationship just because the man makes the first move or never to call a man again. I'm only telling you not to stress yourself out trying to analyze a man's every move. Let the man pursue you and then you don't have to worry if he is really interested. Trust me, he will show you by his actions.

Take Abigail, for example. She had high goals in life she wanted to achieve. She was twenty-five years old, working on her master's in education. Most men would say that she wasn't too bad looking on the eyes. There was this one guy in Abigail's class that she really liked. They were two different people but there was just something about him that captured her attention.

One day after class Abigail went up to him and found out that his name was Eric. He was also working on his master's in education and would be through in a couple of months. Abigail felt a connection right then and there. She immediately asked if she could have his number and if maybe they could study together sometime. So they both exchanged numbers and it seemed to be the start of a beautiful friendship. Abigail could not wait for Eric to call her. Three days went by and she was getting a little impatient. She thought she had felt some kind of spark. Maybe he was just shy, so she thought that she would hurry the process just a little bit. So she decided to call him. They had a pretty good conversation and Abigail asked him if he would like to go to lunch with her sometime. Eric said that he would and he would call her later but he really had to go.

She waited a couple of days for him to call her back but she didn't hear anything. She did not want to seem desperate so she decided to text him. After ten minutes, Eric responded back that he was hanging out with friends but that he would text her later. She waited but he never texted her back. She thought that maybe he forgot to text her back. She texted him to make sure he didn't forget. Abigail was not used to men being as shy as Eric. She really wanted to go out with him, so she decided to make the first move again. So she called him.

"Hey, what's up? I didn't mean to bother you. It was getting late and I was about to go to bed. I just wanted to know if you wanted to go to lunch with me tomorrow. I know this small sandwich shop off campus that is really cheap but they sell the best sandwiches."

"Umm. Yeah. Tomorrow is not good for me. I have homework and I have to work," Eric said.

"Well, what days are you off? Maybe we can work around your schedule and see what is good for you. Only if you want to," Abigail said.

"I get off at 10, mostly every night. I'm off on Wednesdays. So it probably would have to be sometime after 6." Eric yawned.

"Okay, great. Let's meet at, say, 6:45, and we can eat dinner and talk about class." Abigail bit her lip trying to hide her excitement.

"Sounds good. Just call me." Eric yawned again.

"Excuse me. I'm getting tired. I'm going to bed now but just call me Wednesday." Eric yawned a the third time.

"Okay, I will. Get some sleep. Goodnight." Abigail said with a big smile on her face.

"Nite." Eric hung up.

Abigail got off the phone smiling and in a very good mood. She could not believe that Eric was so shy. She could see now that she was going to have to make the first moves. She decided that she did not mind because he was worth it. On Wednesday, Abigail called Eric to see if they were still meeting. He did not answer his phone when she called him the first two times. She thought that he said that he was off on Wednesdays. *Maybe he was busy,* she thought. It was going on 5:30 and Eric didn't call her to say that they were still meeting. She decided to text Eric to see if they were still on for their dinner. She knew that he might not have been able to answer the phone if he were busy. But certainly he could text her so she could know something. Eric did not text her back till 6:15. He did not say anything about lunch. It was a simple "Hey, how are you doing?" Abigail came to the conclusion that Eric just forgot or he was trying not to seem too excited or dorky. So she texted him back and asked if they were still meeting at 6:45. He texted her back saying that he had forgot but that they could still meet.

Abigail was excited but a little discouraged because Eric seemed like he really didn't want to meet her. She shrugged off her feelings and just decided that he was having a bad day and needed cheering up. She rushed to the sandwich shop to wait for him. He arrived five minutes late. Abigail did most of the talking while Eric listened. Whenever she asked him a question, he would respond in less than three sentences. Abigail was beginning to think they were too different. He was so shy and reserved. She did not know why she thought that they had so much in common. Just then, a girl walked by and Eric called her name. He seemed really excited to talk to her as she came to the table and gave him a hug. He didn't stop smiling once. They talked for at least ten minutes before the girl blushed, asking if she was interrupting anything. Eric made a face and waved the comment off.

"Hey, Abigail, this is Tanya. Tanya, this is Abigail, she's in one of my classes. We were just discussing some of our class assignments. So whatever happened to you, did you graduate with your PhD in business yet?" Eric smiled at her.

"No, not yet. I am thinking of going back one day. I'm really just working at a bank right now." Tanya blushed.

"Hey, I'd like to catch up with you some time. Do you have a number where I can reach you?" Eric searched his pockets for a piece of paper.

"Hey, Abigail, do you have a pencil or pen in your pocketbook?" Eric asked.

Abigail tried to hide her frustration. This was a totally different Eric than the one that had been speaking to her. She couldn't get him to say more than three words. Then Tanya walks in and he couldn't keep his mouth shut. She came to the conclusion that Eric was not shy. He just wasn't that in to her.

There is nothing wrong with starting a conversation with a guy or going out to lunch with him. Remember, in order to really know if a guy is into you, you have to let him make the first move. Abigail was the one making all the moves while Eric wasn't making any. She was doing all the calling and the texting. Eric was simply responding back to her texts and phone calls. She thought he was shy so she really didn't consider the fact that Eric wasn't really into her. Abigail noticed he seemed to be interested in Tanya. Tanya didn't have to ask Eric whether he wanted her number. He automatically asked for her number with no hesitation. When a guy is really into you, he beats you to all the punches. He is interested in you so he calls you. He returns your texts without you being the only one putting in all the work. If a guy is really into you, trust me you'll know it!

OOPS, I FELL!

There is nothing wrong with falling and making mistakes. To be truthful, everybody makes mistakes. It only becomes a disadvantage when we keep making the same mistake over and over again. Some women you talk to date the same type of man over and over. If she did not say each man's name, you would think that she was talking about the same man. Each man has a different name but the same personality and behavior patterns. All the men that she dates may all even look alike. You may be laughing right now because you know two or three friends who do this.

It is important that after every relationship, we have some time to reflect. Reflecting allows women to see patterns in their old relationships that they should look out for in their future ones. Look back over your relationships and take an assessment of what traits each man had in common. Then in the future, look for a man that does not have those traits. I do not suggest reflecting too long. Reflecting over anything that is painful is not healthy. The key to positive and effective reflection is to gather helpful information and discard the rest. Look at just enough information to form patterns and draw conclusions.

Do not make decisions when you are hurt, bitter, emotional, or angry. There is nothing wrong with a woman's emotions. It's only when we rely strictly on our emotions that we get into trouble. Sometimes it's easy to want to hurry and date another guy because we are hurting. It's easy to never want to date another man again because all men are so-called dogs.

I'm not telling you not to feel the pain or admit that it is there. What I am saying is not to hold on to the pain when making a decision. Try to do something to take your mind off the emotion. When feeling emotional, try cleaning, running, squeezing a stress ball, punching a boxing bag, or jump roping. Any of these actions will help to get that aggressive energy out.

Sometimes it may seem like it's easier to hold on to pain than letting it go. It hurts when we try to move on and we get rejected again. The first thought that pops into our mind is, *Why did I let my guard down? I knew he was going to hurt me just like the other men did.* Don't be foolish, but do not anticipate that every man is going to hurt you. Your mind has a lot of power. Our attitude (frame of mind) sets how our whole day will go. Don't think of negative things every day and every second. Turn your fear into courage by saying, "I am going to meet the right man. I may be scared but I deserve to be happy."

Don't be like the woman who stayed in her house all day because she thought all men would hurt her. She constantly cried every night. She would write in her diary every day about the no-good men in the world. She dreamed of men who would use her. She thought about all the men that ever hurt her. One day the woman passed by a mirror in her house. She screamed and ran toward the door. Suddenly she stopped and slowly approached the mirror again. She could not believe it. The face that stared back at her was the face of an old woman. What happened to the youthful and joyful woman she had once been? The woman moped around the house for many days.

One day, the woman had a dream that she would meet a man. She could not explain the dream but she began to become curious. Out of the blue, she felt an urge to go outside. She decided that she could not stay in the house for the rest of her life. She could not prevent what was going to happen. For the first time in fifteen years, she stepped out of her house into the sun. At first, the brightness hurt her eyes. But as she walked, she became used to the light.

She sat down next to a man sitting on a park bench, reading the daily paper. She cleared her throat and said in a loud voice,

"You do not know me but my name is Fear." The startled man looked up from his paper and extended his hand to Fear.

"Hello, I am Worry. I've heard a lot about you. I am curious. What made you become courageous enough to come out today?" The woman kept staring ahead as he spoke.

"I've decided that I can't stop life from happening; the only thing I managed to stop...was my life." Fear wiped a falling tear from her check.

"Miss, I know what you mean. I've been sitting here for ten years to meet you. Anytime, I would have gotten up to do something and then we might not have met."

BABY'S STEPS CAN GO A LONG WAY

Never be afraid to take baby steps in a relationship. There is nothing wrong with falling and getting back up. Most babies fall a couple of times before they learn how to walk. Falling is not a bad thing. It teaches us to get back up. What if babies never got back up after they fell down? They would still be sitting in the same place ten years from now. It's okay if you fell a few times. Get back up and strut your stuff. Take your time. Take small steps before you give your heart away again. It's okay to slowly walk into a relationship. There is nothing wrong with that as long as you don't come to a complete stop. Keep moving. Keep feeling. Always keep your joy no matter who is around or not.

Sometimes when women are hurting, they have to find a reason why the man left or why it did not work out before they are able to move on. Women will turn to relationship books, articles, and their friends for advice. While you may find some useful information, most of the time the answers keep you trapped mentally in the relationship. You start to make excuses and go into the psychology of why it did not work out. These may be some of the reasons that you feel the relationship did not work out:

1. He never knew his mom or they did not have a good relationship. He is really taking his frustration out on you because he never had a good relationship with his mom and he is not used to a woman loving him. He does not feel like he deserves it, that is why he does not return love when you give it to him. He does not want you to leave because it reminds him of the broken relationship that he had with his mom. And when you leave it reminds him of that broken bond. Give him time and he will began to love you back the way you need him too. But you have to be patient with him because he is wounded.

   This man may have had issues with his mom but he cannot live right now by referring to the past. He has a woman that is willing to love him right now (you). If he wants to have a relationship with his mom or forgive her, then they should both go to counseling. If he doesn't want to go to counseling then he is saying that he does not want to remember the past so he needs to let it go. He doesn't need permission to treat someone wrong because he can't let the past go. We have all been through things but we cannot use them as excuses to live recklessly or treat people wrong. When a criminal hurts someone, he cannot blame it on the fact that he is mad. He has to be held accountable, serve time, and get counseling if he is mentally unstable. Know that he does not have a good relationship with his mom but also know that he has to want to be able to heal before it can actually happen.

2. He saw his dad cheat and he is repeating that pattern of what he learned. He never saw a positive example of a good relationship, thus he is scared to get into one. He never knew that he could fall in love. That is why he played so many women because he did not know that good and happy relationships exist.

We cannot give other people power to influence our behavior. Because once our actions are done, we cannot say "They made me do it," because we control our bodies, words, and actions. Counseling is not a bad idea if you have something that you cannot handle. If a man is not seeking help in learning to be responsible for his own actions, then he risks being under the control of other people.

3. He is scared to fall in love because a woman hurt him so bad before. He is scared to give his heart away and trust women again. He doesn't trust any woman because he is afraid that she'll hurt him like the last one did.

   We have all been hurt but that does not give us a right to pass that hurt on. He needs to heal before he moves into the next relationship so that he can separate his past and his present. If he cannot do this, then maybe he should talk to someone so that they can help him deal with the pain. If he is not willing to do this, then he needs to let it go before it destroys any future relationships he might have.

4. When men start feeling like the woman is the one for them, they start to feel trapped and need to get out of the relationship or cheat to relieve the pressure of feeling trapped. Men only start to feel this when they are with the right woman and they are afraid of commitment and getting married.

   Men feel this when they do not want to commit. You are not asking for marriage right now. You are asking him to be a boyfriend. If he does not want to commit to women, then he should not be having sex with you. He should not be in a relationship with you and he should be friends and let you move on. If he does not want to do this, then he wants to have his cake and eat it too, and he is making excuses to do that.

5. When he says that he needs space, he really does not want space. He just wants to play games with you. He wants you to chase him, but he is scared to ask you to fight for his love. So therefore, you have to win his love back and show him that you will be there for him and deserve to be in his life.

A man that does not know what he wants is a dangerous man. This type of man never wants to commit to any one person. So before you let him get away with that excuse, be sure that you do not mind waiting years and never knowing true and consistent love.

6. You didn't give enough in the beginning. You have to give your all and put up with a lot of things in relationships to show your man that he can trust you. If he feels like you were not there for him a lot of times, he feels like he is scared to open up until he feels like he can trust you.

Well, what does he have to give you? Relationships are not supposed to be lopsided. They're supposed to be equal. No one person should feel like they are doing all of the work. If both people are working, then no one notices if the other one isn't.

7. You were too emotional and men do not understand emotion because they are so logical. You need to be cooler and not nag him as much, or he will want to leave.

I do not believe in nagging a man, but if there is something that he is doing that you do not agree with, please do not keep silent. If a man is going to leave because you have morals or you want to voice your opinion then maybe he should go.

8. What you won't do, another woman will. If your man likes oral sex and you do not give it to him, then you are telling and giving your man permission to go somewhere else. What you won't do in the bedroom, another woman will.

If a guy bases his relationship with you on your sex life instead of things like morals and character, then let him go. You can always find another man, but they say they have not found a cure for AIDS. Any man that will leave you because you did not have oral sex with him or because your freak meter is not amped to a level ten is not worth staying with.

9. You were too clingy and emotional. He did not know how to take it and that is why he cheated. He should talk to you and tell you that you are being emotional and clingy and that that pushes him away. Real men will tell you they do not like this. Any man that says that pushed him to cheat is not a real man. This lets you know that when times get tough, this man will cheat. He doesn't have to like you being clingy or emotional. You both should talk it out so you can change that. He should come to an understanding of where you both want to go in the relationship. If it is not working, then be friends.

It's not that being clingy and emotional made him cheat. It's how he chose to handle it. He could have talked to you first or broke it off if it was not working. Don't go back because you feel like you made him cheat. Go back because you want to work it out for you, if that is what you chose to do.

All of these reasons make it easier for the man to come back in your life. Through these, you have given him excuses as to why the relationship did not work out and why you should take him back again. And then you're even more depressed because nothing has changed, and instead, things seem worse. Now he sees you twice a week instead of once a week. He used to talk to you on the phone often, but he has cut that out because in his mind he sees you more. You're still not happy and when you complain about it, he brings up the excuse you provided him with. You then feel like you should stay because you have been through too much together and you begin to just think breaking up and getting back together is normal. You get used to him being there and you can't see your world without him in it, even if you are unhappy. Every time you leave, you come back because it's a pattern that has been going on for so long.

WHEN THINGS CHANGE

What happens when you are not trying to catch a man? You're just trying to keep the one that you have. You wonder where the spark went that was so alive in the beginning of the relationship. You don't know if he is cheating or he just does not care anymore. You have been in the relationship for a little while with this man and you are not happy anymore. You want to end the relationship, but you do love him. You may have children with this man or have been in the relationship for a long time that you feel you do not want to be with anyone else. You want to work things out, but you have noticed so many signs you don't even know if the relationship can be saved:

1. He's happy to get off the phone. You barely talk fifteen minutes a day.

2. The relationship is not exciting anymore. The guy feels like he knows you and that he doest not have to work that hard to be romantic anymore.

3. You ask him how the relationship is going and he says that he thinks everything is good. You get upset because you cannot believe that he does not realize how unhappy you are.

4. He tends to use quick fixes for permanent and serious problems. You tell him something is wrong and he changes for three days, and then it seems like everything is back to the way that it used to be again.

5. He doesn't appreciate you, and oftentimes, it seems like you do more for him than he for you.

6. When it is time to be intimate, it seems like he is just going through the motions. You cannot feel the care or love in the act.

7. You rarely go out anymore. You may go out once a month or every two weeks. And that is because you have begged and may have even withheld sex from him. So he feels like he must make an exchange to get what you are withholding from him.

8. He has stopped telling you that you look nice and complimenting you on dates. You may even have started giving you criticism about your hair, your makeup, your cooking, and your appearance lately.

9. When he talks to you, there is a lack of emotion in his voice.

10. When he does talk longer to you, it is after you both have had a disagreement and he always wants to have sex once he gives it a little time. Then he goes back to almost ignoring you again.

11. It seems like he wants to avoid talking to you and spending time with you altogether.

12. He says that you nag whenever he talks to you, and that is why he doesn't talk to you anymore.

13. You get into an argument almost every day.

14. He stops buying you anything.

15. He forgets your birthday, anniversary, and sad to say, even Valentine's Day. He seems hesitant to go out on that day and to even buy you a gift. He may not have totally forgotten about the day, but his lack of preparations makes you feel like he might as well as have forgotten.

16. He seems distant when he is with you. His body is there but you can tell that his mind is somewhere else.

17. He is constantly looking at other women. This does not mean that he is cheating; he may just be looking only. He does this on the sly, but you still notice that he is looking at other women. It always seems to be a certain type of woman that he looks at. They all have the same features, the same skin type, the same length of hair and the same body type.

18. He gets upset with you about everything easily.

19. He only wants to see you and spend time with you when it is convenient for him.

20. He forgets things about you that you have reminded him of before.

21. He is always sleepy when you want to get on the phone and talk to him.

22. He calls you when he is bored. He may even promise to call you back later but always forgets. You have to call him back which makes it seem like you are needy.

23. When he watches TV, he constantly tells you how fine the woman on the TV is. When you confront him, he tells you that she is on TV. You can't get mad because he will never be able to be with her or cheat with someone on the TV.

24. He cusses a lot around you and he talks about going to the bathroom all the time. It's like he feels so comfortable around you to the point that he is not even trying to impress you anymore.

25. He always talks about the same things and never asks about your day or your thoughts like he did in the beginning of the relationship.

26. He spends more time with his friends and strangers than he does with you.

27. You become the last one to know anything about him. He will tell everyone else and then you find out through them or by mistake.

28. Every time you have an argument, he talks to his friends and family and not with you. He acts like he does not want to talk with you or everything is cool until someone tells you what he says.

29. He starts to take you to dirty places to eat when you do go out, and it is always takeout. He never wants to dine anymore.

30. He tells you that the decision is yours to make, but when you suggest anything, it always ends up being his choice.

31. He picks the movies or he does not want to go.

32. He makes it seem like he is unhappy in the relationship, but when you give him a choice to leave and be happy, he does not want to go anywhere. You wonder if he is playing games or just trying to get his way by making it seem like he puts up with you.

33. He does not dress up when he goes out with you anymore. He wears dirty tennis shoes or old clothes with stains in them. Strangers see him in new clothes more than you do. You notice he dresses up more when he does not go out with you.

34. You are very unhappy in the relationship and find yourself eating when you are not hungry.

35. When you do not answer his calls, it's like he does not notice anymore. He used to be possessive and wonder why you missed his call. Now if you do not answer, you only see

one missed call on your phone or none at all. He may not call you again until the next day.

36. It seems like he is not at home like he used to be. You call but no one answers, and when he does call you back, it is late or the day after. It is always an excuse.

37. When you call him, he takes the longest time to call you back.

38. You may have noticed new stuff around his place and you wonder if someone else is buying it for him. You do not want to start an argument. Things are already not going so good, but you get the strange feeling another woman bought it.

39. He seems to want to keep you distracted. It seems like he purposely leaves things in your car or in his car for you to go get for him. It's like he wants you to leave, so that he can do something without you knowing. Every time he does this, he is either on the phone or getting off the phone when you come back.

40. You notice he does not answer calls when he is with you. The person calls twice or thrice, and they do not answer the phone.

41. He always has to go to the bathroom several times when you are out on dates. He says he has to use the bathroom or wash his hands before he eats. It's always after he receives a text message or a missed call that he does not answer in front of you.

42. He walks really fast like he does not want to walk with you when you go places together.

43. He acts like he is not interested in having sex with you anymore. Some books will have you to believe that a man's sex drive increases for you when he is cheating. The reasoning behind it is that he does not want you to

know that he is cheating. I'm not going to say there is no truth to that but most women that have suspicions about men cheating complain of a decrease in their men's sexual appetites toward them. One of the first signs that worry a woman that a man is cheating is that he doesn't seems to want to have sex with her as much as he used to. That is not to say that he never will have sex with her again. She just notices that weeks go by and he doesn't seem bothered that he is not getting any from her when this would have made him go crazy before. So if he is not getting it from her, she wonders where else he could be getting it from.

44. He suddenly spends a lot of time at work, hanging out with his buddy, dancing at the club, or gambling.

45. He always makes you feel like the bad guy. He can say that you do not talk to him anymore, and then when you do, you always say the wrong things. You can want to have sex and he says you want it too much, or you can want it less and he will say that you don't want him anymore. It does not matter what you do, as he always finds a way to complain about anything that you are doing.

46. You notice that he smells too good lately. Sometimes he does not wear any cologne for a while. Then all of a sudden, he begins to wear cologne like it is going out of style. Men may have a favorite scent that they war all the time. You know it because it is the only scent that they wear. That is okay, but it only becomes suspicious when they do things that vary from their usual patterns. One of the reasons men get caught so easily in cheating than women is that men will break their normal patterns. Men are not like women who constantly like change and variety. Most men do not like change and the only time they change is when the store stops carrying a certain brand that they have

worn for years. So that is one of the most crucial signs a woman should look for.

47. You notice that he smells too good. Is he trying to cover up something? You do not want him smelling bad but you notice that every time he is with you he always has to take a shower first. You notice he wants to smell really good for you like he is afraid you might smell another woman's scent on him.

48. You notice he is into eating at new places all of a sudden. He likes to experience new things that he has never done before that are outside his habits. A lot of times when you meet someone new, you enter their world and usually get accustomed to their tastes whether you realize it or not. Friends may say that you have changed and that since you've met this new person, you don't act the same. You may argue that you have not changed until you really start to think about it. It is the same thing for men; they do not notice that they are changing when they are. You can't help it when you meet someone new. A lot of times when a person's tastes change from when you meet them, they are dating someone new.

49. He actually says that he needs cologne as well as new shoes and clothes. This signifies a need for him to impress someone else. Remember that he dressed up with you in the beginning. You saw him in new shoes and clothes and he smelled really nice. He might have stopped doing it as much when you got together. There might have been times when you saw him in his work clothes or just plain clothes. His need for new stuff all of a sudden is a sign that he needs to impress someone else, especially if he buys these new things but he is not wearing them around you.

50. He made excuses about where he would be and why he couldn't see you. He forgot he told you he was at a certain

place and says he hasn't been there in a while. He may even have said another place's name instead. When people lie then they forget what they said after some time. So if you find discrepancies in the places that he says that he is going to be, then he is hiding something.

51. You notice that he never has any money. You know that he has to pay for gas, groceries, bills, and other things. But he will tell you that he had two hundred dollars and in days or a week, it is gone. Every woman has learned if her man is cheap or if he is a spender. So if your man is cheap and you notice that he will tell you he has a specific amount and then he only has fifty dollars, something is wrong. You have to ask yourself if this money is going to drugs, gambling, hotels, or other women.

52. When he talks to you, he stutters, clears his throat, or seems nervous, especially when you ask him questions about where he has been or if he is cheating. Every man is different, but when a man gets nervous, he always has something that he does every single time like clockwork. You can even tell him that he does it and he will deny it and still do it without knowing that he is doing it. He may clear his throat when he lies or bite his nails. He may even shake his leg or move uncomfortably. Whatever he does, look for consistent patterns that he does when he lies. Some men are such good liars that they hardly move when they lie so you cannot detect anything from them when they lie. A lot of times, if a man does not show it in his body language, you can tell it in his voice. His tone seems to go higher and his story will sound too perfect like he rehearsed it in his mind several times before actually saying it to you. Never rely on just one clue to tell if a man is lying or if his story does not sound right. Do not go looking for evidence to find him guilty but do not overlook none either.

Right now, you are probably remembering the times in the beginning of the relationship when he did not mind waking up to talk to you. He brought you little gifts and made time for you in his schedule. It did not matter what time it was; he just wanted to see you. He wanted to take you out to eat and go catch the latest movies. He even said the most romantic things and now it seems like all he needs are three things:

1. Sex—He doesn't take you out anymore; he just tells you that he needs it.

2. Food—He wants to know what you cooked today and he needs to know that before he has sex with you

3. Money—He goes to work and he just wants to relax after a stressful day. Maybe you feel hurt because it seems like you both could de-stress together, but it seems like he finds you to be one of the things that are stressing him.

Should you leave or even try to make this work? You may be confused, but this is how you decide what to do. If you find five to seven things from the above list that you need to work on in your relationship, then stay. Even if you find ten things, you should still try to make it work. I mean no relationship is going to be perfect. It is always going to be a continuous process for both people to keep things exciting and romantic. But if there are thirty or more things from the above list that you relate to, then it may be time to let it go. That is just too many problems. That means that he does not care and he knows that you will put up with anything. If you feel your relationship is worth keeping, the following chapter discusses several ideas that will spice things up a bit.

KEEPING THE RELATIONSHIP ALIVE: WATER TAKES THE FIRE OUT!

Keep the fire burning! Water and fire do not mix!

If you are at this section in the book, then I want to warn you that the effects can be somewhat romantic and very satisfying. If you are currently not in a relationship, then you can read this section at a later time. If you are in a place where you are trying to end a bad relationship, then read this section anyway. It will help you decide if your relationship is in a romantic place or if it has been run over by a truck. Whenever you decide to read this section, keep in mind that you do not have to follow these ideas to the precise word. Feel free to adapt them to your taste and get creative. Who knows, they may even spark a few ideas of your own. Here are a few ideas to keep the flame burning.

We all know that water is one of the fastest ways to kill a fire. Water and fire simply do not mix. Sometimes in a relationship, it is easy for water to kill that flame that was once burning strong.

What extinguishes a lot of flames is the fact that you get to a point in the relationship where you think, "This is it. I've been with this person for a while and we had all of our excitement. The only thing to do now is just watch TV together." There is certainly nothing wrong with that. But you have not reached your limit in the relationship; you can go further. Don't be afraid to try something new and do something different. You don't even have to spend a lot of money to be romantic or have a good time. All a romantic date requires is two willing partners, love, and a really big imagination.

It is important that you never look at someone else's relationship and compare it to yours. Everybody is different. So of course, every relationship is going to be different. You have the right to do things in your own relationship that make you and your partner happy. Most importantly, I want you to embrace the idea of spending money from the heart. The time and thought that you put into your dates is what's really valuable. Let's explore some examples of what I mean:

- **Dancing Under Balloons**

   Go to a romantic place where it will just be the two of you. Blow up balloons and push little notes inside of them before you tie a knot in the balloon. The notes can say how much you love that person. You can write down anything you want to say. The point of releasing the balloons into the sky is to express your love for one another or just to say something good about your relationship. Bring a boom box and dance under the balloons that you both released into the sky. It can be as many balloons as you want, or it can just be a single balloon. The balloons will eventually pop and there is no telling where they will end up. This is okay because you want someone to find your romantic notes to let other people know that dreams do come true.

- **Date at the Dollar Tree**

   Blind fold your date and tell them that you have a surprise for them. When you get to the Dollar Tree or (any store with really low priced items in it), say "Tah-dah!" They will probably look at you with a confused expression that says "You have got to be kidding." That's when you tell them that this is only part of the date. You and your sweetie should pick out five items out of the dollar tree that remind you of each other. For example, he could choose a candle for you because you light up his life. On your part, you could choose a box of Kleenex tissues, because he's there for you whenever you are sad. Don't let the other person see what you have bought until dinner or after your date. When you sit down in the restaurant to eat your dinner, show each other the items. Tell each other why you choose these items and how your sweetie influenced the items you bought. The other person gets to keep the items that you bought to describe them. This is just a fun way to tell the other person how you feel about them by showing them.

- **Teddy Bear Surprise**

  The teddy bear is a representation of you. There should be something special inside of the teddy that is only for them. Only the person that has your heart can find it. Inside of the teddy bear should be a hollow place or an opening that fits a small surprise in its storage compartment. Some bears may already have an opening in the back to store things. With some bears, you can build and stuff them yourself. In the place where you would stuff them (put enough stuffing so that your bear is not flat), place your secret item inside the bear. Most "build your own bears" are not expensive. You can find them in small toy stores or in the toy sections of department stores. The bear does not have to cost a lot.

- **Indoor Camping**

  Camping can be anywhere that you would like it to be. Most camping trips allow people to spend time together. Well maybe you are not a person that enjoys nature a lot. That is okay because you can bring nature to you. You can set up a tent inside your house.

  Here are some of the necessary jtems you would need:

  1. Blankets
  2. Fan (tie strips or yarn to front of fan)
  3. Yellow and red strips of paper or yarn.
  4. S'mores candy bars
  5. Potable radio ran by batteries

6. Scary camp stories

7. Set plants or pictures of animals around tent

The purpose of indoor camping is to spend time together. You can do this in a familiar and comfortable but creative setting. You can camp out in the yard or actually in the wild. Whatever you decide to do, just remember to bring fun along with you and watch out for itchy plants!

- **Public announcement**

    Before you take this idea to heart, make sure that this idea will not embarrass your partner. The purpose of this idea is to let the world know that you are not ashamed of him, but that you are very proud to be with him and you want to share this feeling with others. You can take this person out to eat, to the mall, or any other public place. The announcement does not have to be long. You just want to make sure that others know what a wonderful boyfriend you have. It's good to let people know how much you appreciate them by the little things that you do. Sometimes hearing the appreciation is just as good. Have fun!

- **Outdoor movie**

    Pick a day when the weather man says it is going to be sunny and have a movie date. Bring snacks or popcorn to eat as you watch your movie on your laptop or portable DVD player. Lay a blanket on the ground and enjoy the picture show. If you prefer, you can replace the movie with outdoor dancing. Just bring a radio and some CDs and dance outside. Of course, you can choose a private spot where it is just you and your partner. The point of the date is that you spend time together and get to know one another all over again.

- **Date Collage**

  Take your date on an exciting trip and do not forget to bring your camera. The purpose of the date is to go to a place that you have never been before. Take pictures of the two of you enjoying the scenery and the day's activities. When the date is over, be sure to use your minds to create a masterpiece. Get together and make a mini scrapbook of the experience. Both of you can write sentences under the picture that remind you of the day you had together. Or you can surprise your partner with the mini-scrapbook on his birthday. You can write down your own memories under the photos and leave a space for him to write down his. You can also make a mini–slide show for him if you have a digital camera and the software on your computer. The date collage is just a way to capture good memories on paper and in your heart.

- **First Date Movie Premier**

  Get your best buds together and do a reenactment of your first date. If you had some hilarious moments, then have your buds act out that scene. Or you can do a scene that captures what you loved about your boyfriend. For example, if he pulled out your chair at one point, you can make a side comment into the camera that you were hooked at that moment. If you had on something nice, then get the male bud that is playing your boyfriend to say into the camera something like you couldn't get any more beautiful than you were that night. There are a lot of things that you can do with this movie. The power of the camera is yours!

- **The Book of You**

  The Book of You is to capture facts about your boyfriend that he didn't think you remembered. The book doesn't have to be a hundred pages. It can be as minimal as ten pages. The point of the booklet is just to let him know that you have been listening all along. Your book can contain memorable photos and details about your boyfriend's favorite foods and hobbies. You can even list their dreams and goals in life. The Book of You is a fun way to see your partner in a new light. They will appreciate the booklet because of the time and effort you put into it.

- **Special Moment Prom**

  Remember prom in high school. Well, it's back! You are not in high school any longer but you have entered the school of life. You have been through some rough breakups. You have had some bad and good experiences with dating. Well, there comes a time in every woman's life that she enters her special moment prom. This night is to celebrate your victories with not giving up on the school of love. You have had some setbacks but you still kept your faith in love. The special person you are with is just one reward of not giving up after heartbreak. Hey, if you didn't keep going, then you would not be with that person today. Be proud of your accomplishments. You can have a prom setup in the backyard or indoors if you want. Invite your closest friends over to have a good time, eat, and play fun games. They can choose to dress up (as if you were really at a prom) or you can set the dress code for a more casual theme. Have some friends dress up as chaperones or waiters who serve you and your friends during the party. Put up white and silver balloons or any pattern you want to. Hang banners and have fun door prizes for your guests. It's your party and you can get as creative as you want.

- **Tasting World Cuisines**

  Have a night set up where you bring a specific country and its culture to your place. Whether you are in the mood for Chinese or Mexican, bring it to your place. Set up a table with the theme of the country and prepare different foods from that place. To make it even more fun, blindfold your partner and let him guess what food he is eating. You can make a game out of it. For each answer he gets correct, he can get tickets. These tickets can be cashed in for a prize. I'm going to leave it right there because I want your imagination to get working. I do not want to limit your creativity. The whole point of the evening is to experience something new and spend time together. The food that you buy can even be his favorite food. Be creative but remember to have fun.

- **Roses in a Mirror**

  Purposely send your partner only eleven roses. Make sure that he knows there should be twelve in all. Attach a note to each rose; each note should lead to the next rose. On the eleventh note, tell him that the twelfth rose is priceless and this rose you want to keep. Let the note lead to the mirror. You can even tape large stems to the mirror to add more of an effect. When he looks into the mirror, he will realize that he is the twelfth rose.

- **Intellect of the Poet**

  You and your partner can play a fun game that involves both of you using your minds. Place a certain quantity of items on the floor. Record yourselves and make a poem that consists of so many lines. The items on the floor can give inspiration or you can actually talk about the items themselves. The point of the game is to get your minds to spend time with each other. A lot of times, couples get so comfortable with each other they eventually spend time together in silence. This exercise will allow you both to be creative while exercising your mouth at the same time.

- **CD Mixer**

  Make a CD with your boyfriend's favorite songs on it. Play it and dance to it when the two of you are alone.

You can add a nice twist to this idea by dancing in a pool. You can have roses in the water and candles around the pool. The point of the evening is to do something fun in a different way. It will be exciting and a good way for you both to laugh and create new memories.

- **Doing what you love**

  It is also very important to spend time doing the things that you both love to do. Find some activity that you both have in common and spend time doing this activity. It could be painting, drawing, writing, or listening to music. Whatever the activity is, just have fun and do it together.

- **Promise Vows**

  Promise vows are a way of renewing your love for each other. You can do this when you are alone. The purpose of the evening is just to let the other person know how you feel. You can videotape this evening and you both can dress up if you want to. Have soft music playing with roses or petals surrounding both of you. You can have candles lit and soft fragrances filling the room. Tell each other how you feel. You can write a poem or sing a special song that you have made for each other. Make it a special evening that you and your boyfriend can play back over and over in your heart.

- **Love Language**

  You and your boyfriend can make up love signs or a love language only you both know. Use your fingers and hands together to make signs that mean something to you. Nobody should know what the language means. This enables you to be in a crowded room and tell each other how you feel without using your lips. It's fun because it adds one more way to say "I love you" or "I care."

- **Candlelit Setting on the Floor**

  Be very careful not to burn the place down. Maybe you want to replace the candles and batteries for a laser light device that you plug in the wall. You can turn the setting to slow so that different colored patterns light the wall and give your surroundings a magical effect. Lay a picnic blanket on the floor and cook your favorite meal. You can have the song that you both met to playing in the background, or maybe you want to set the TV on the floor with a couple of pillows and a blanket and make it a movie night with lots of cuddling. The purpose of this theme is to get into a place wherein you can rekindle the moment that made you both fall in love. You can play a fun game called Love or Be Loved. In this game, you both have to think of words that describe the other (you can make it sexy, funny or romantic). You may even have to remember fun facts like the other person's favorite food, movie, or color. The purpose of the game and the whole evening is to fall in love with each other again. Who says that you are only allowed to fall once?

- Now take it from here and start thinking of some ideas of your own that will help liven things up in your relationship. But if you have read this part and you are in tears because you feel your relationship is unfixable, move on to the next section.

FREE YOURSELF: BEGIN TO BREAK

If you are not happy in the relationship, do not stay in it just because you have invested years of your life. A lot of times women stay because they feel like they have been through so much with this one person. Really, you have been through too much. The longer you stay in this relationship, the harder it is to let it go.

Before you leave you have to make for sure that you are ready because otherwise, you will always come back to him whether you want to or not. Sometimes it is easy to let it go. You know what you want to do and you do it. You may come back one more time and after it does not work the second time, you are through. A lot of times, it does not work that way. You may have went back several times and said you would not go back after each time. It seems like no matter what you do, you cannot get away from this man that you feel so unhappy with.

First before you leave, make a list that contains two columns. Do not let this list dictate your life by any means. The list is mainly for you to see all the pros and cons of being in a relationship with your man. If the list has more cons than pros, then you may want to talk with your man to discuss whether he is willing to change or if he can risk losing you. If he is willing to change, then work it out. If not then prepare yourself to slowly break away from him.

Sometimes cutting someone off is not an easy process. It's not like you can directly say, "I'm not going to talk, listen, or have sex with you anymore." A man will not take you seriously if you keep on breaking up with him but take him back just as easily. He will not make any serious effort to change because he knows you are not really serious about your threats.

Let's look at some important steps that you can take to help you break away from someone and eventually move on:

1. Reduce the sex. You may not be able to cut it off completely. Men know how to get back in with a woman. He whispers the sweetest poetry in her ear to break her down. He reminds her of the good memories they used to have and then the last thing he does is touch her and kiss her so that she remembers the sex. For women, it is not so much the feeling that they miss but the bond that they share with the man. When the woman slowly comes back and when he is comfortable that she is in his hands again, he

goes back to his old ways. She is not happy but she cannot leave now because her emotions have become invested in the relationship again. So she stays because she may not have found any one that really knows her like he does. Whether he is taking advantage of her or not, she still feels like this man knows her emotionally, mentally, and physically. Women get comfortable too in relationships just like men. She knows this man. They have shared so much and she is not sure she can leave. Physically she can, but mentally and emotionally, she knows that he has her and that is what prevents her from leaving physically.

2. Don't spend as much time with him. Do not give all of your time to one person. That way, you do not become too dependent on them. Men have mastered this concept. One of the issues women have with men is their lack of time for her. He may give her a day here and two days there but they keep the majority of the time for their selves. And if you notice something, men do not fall as hard as women do. So if we have not learned anything else today, we have at least learned to "not put all of your eggs in one basket." If they break up with you, what are you left with?

    Start doing things by yourself. When you're alone, it's hard to think about going to the movies; eating out; going to concerts, plays, and recitals; bowling; walking in the park; playing at the arcade and amusement park; going to the beach; attending parties, gatherings, and double dates, and going on vacations. Then you don't leave because you start thinking about all the things that you have to start doing by yourself and you get sad. You know he treats you wrong but you know you do not want to start doing all of these things by yourself. The first step in breaking his hold is to show him that you can do things by yourself and have fun. If you are not comfortable going out to eat by yourself, take things slow and start off with going to a movie by yourself. Have you really wanted to see a movie but ended up not seeing it because you did not have any one to go with you? Well, this is one of the steps to breaking the need to having the wrong man in your life because you feel like you will have to do stuff alone if you get rid of him. Go to a movie alone. Or go out to eat alone and bring a book or a cross word puzzle with you. Or some work even to keep you from thinking that you have to have someone with you. You can even ask a sister or a friend to go along with you, but remember that the main goal of going alone is to get used to not being dependent on anyone. Take it slow; maybe you need the support of a friend, sister, or cousin first. Then gradually, you may start to feel independent enough to go to a small diner on your own and sit down and eat. Or maybe you feel more comfortable going to the park and sitting down and having a picnic by yourself instead. Whatever you decide to do, you can have fun just by yourself. Once you do this, you will begin to feel better even without the person. It gives you some time to reflect on whether they are adding happiness to your life or if they are taking more than they are giving.

3. Don't talk as much with him on the phone. The phone is more for the woman than it is the man. After the man has learned a woman, then he wants to talk less on the phone while the woman wants to talk more. Women feel closer to people by emotional and mental connections that they make while talking. Men, on the other hand, may feel closer to people by the time they spend with a person doing things together. So that is one of the reasons why I say that the phone is more for the woman than the man. If you are trying to break this connection with the man, then talking less on the phone will do it. He may have already

broken the connection by wanting to talk less to you on the phone. Do not worry he is actually doing you a favor.

So play it cool and talk less to him each day until you feel less and less of the need to have to talk to him every day or even at all. He will eventually call you more because he is wondering why your patterns have changed. He may even feel like you are moving on, which you are. But do not tell him this because he will only put the game on you and try to sucker you back into staying.

4. Watch his speed. Give only what he does and not more than that. One of the number one complaints of women is they feel like they gave more in a relationship. In the end, they become bitter for it because they felt like they gave their all while the men never gave anything back. There is nothing wrong with doing things from the heart. If you feel like you want to do something for the guy even if he does not do anything for you, do it. But whatever you do, when the relationship is over, do not have any regrets. Give what you know you will not want back even when the relationship ends. Also, you don't want to fall deeply in love with someone that only wants to be friends. You may feel something for the guy but watch to see if he is feeling the same way. Trust me when I say this: Just because you are in love with a guy does not mean he will fall in love with you right back. You don't want to force anything because he will not be happy in the relationship if he feels pressured to feel something that he doesn't. It will eliminate a lot of hurt if women just gave what the man gave in the relationship. If the man is not giving a lot, then don't you give a lot because that means that he really is not into you? He just thinks you are cool to hang out with but he is not trying to give you too much right now. If the guy is making an effort to see you and he's giving just as much as you are, then match his speed, because this

guy knows where he wants to go with you and he wants to make it work. It's okay to give in to this relationship because he is giving.

5. Don't date other men to get over him. What happens when you do this is that you just transfer the pain you feel in your previous relationship on another man. And the situation tends to be worse than the one you came out of. You're hurting and you just need anyone to take the pain away just so you can forget your ex. What you should try to do is learn to become independent so that you whether you are alone or with someone, you can be happy either way. Your happiness is no longer affected by the amount of time a man spends with you but on your choice to be happy with or without him. It is okay to date but only after you have healed and you are truly ready, and you're not just on the rebound from your last relationship. If you are not over the last guy, you will likely attract a guy that reminds you of your ex. For instance, maybe your ex had three kids. You'll then date another guy who has three kids. If the last guy you were with acted a certain way, you'll attract a new guy that does the same thing. You may even attract a guy that resembles the last guy in appearance. So take some time to heal and when you do date again, look for a different guy that does not remind you of the last one. Right now when you're trying to get away from the last guy, you are actually in limbo love. You know that it's better for you if you leave but at the same time you do not want to. Being alone for a while and getting him out of your system is the best thing to do before you move on. What if the next guy is really nice? You cannot be with him fully because you still have feelings for the last guy. So before you move on, take some time to see what you want in life. What are your dreams and likes? You don't need another person to experience happiness. Realizing this

is one of the first steps in freeing yourself from needing someone who is not making you happy.

6. Stop making excuses for a grown man. We all have that complex about mistakes. We know that we all make them and we want to forgive those who hurt us. That is what we are supposed to do for everyone. This is the key that helps you move on: forgiveness. Have you ever heard the expression, "Forgive but don't forget"?

   What this means is that you forgive the person for hurting you so that you can move on. But if a person hurts you not just once but even four consecutive times, do not forget that. See a pattern and get away from this person because they will only keep on doing it as long as you let them. Everybody makes mistakes but we are supposed to learn from our mistakes. Once a mistake is repeated over and over, then it is no longer a mistake. It becomes a pattern which will have a continuous cycle.

   This man is a grown man; let him be accountable for what he does. When you give person accountability for their behavior towards you, it gives your feelings a voice. You're actually saying that you do not hate the person but you do not like how you are being treated; that you deserve better and their behavior is no longer acceptable; that they must change if they want you to continue to be in their; that their negative behavior is affecting your feelings, attitude, and mood. Ask yourself this: if the tables were turned and you were hurting him with your behavior, do you think he would stay? If you were trying to change maybe, but if he saw this was a continuous pattern with you, then maybe he would tell you he could not deal with that and he would leave. You're a human being just like he is, so why would you not do the same?

7. Feel good about yourself and work on boosting your self-confidence. When women opt to stay in bad relationships,

one of the reasons for that could be their low self-esteem. The guy knows that you have low self-esteem and he may feel like you will take any of his mess because you don't have high confidence in yourself. He will walk over you and not think anything about it because he feels like he can. You might have even said it with your words but you did not tell him with your actions.

8. Forgive those who have hurt you. Sometimes we say we have forgiven the men in our past, but we have not. It may not be a boyfriend, a father, an uncle, or a brother that hurt you. Forgive them and move on. You cannot change what happened in the past. If you invent a time machine then you can. But until that happens, you have to work with what you have now which is forgiveness. They have moved on with their lives and they may even have forgotten what they have done. And sometimes they may remember and try to make amends later, but you may be too hurt to see that. Or maybe they are not trying to make amends. Whatever the case, you have to move on and be happy even if you feel like the hurt was too bad to forgive.

9. Go to counseling. We all need someone to talk to. We want to talk to the guy that hurt us, the guy that we are trying to move on from. We want to tell them what we feel and how unhappy we are in the relationship. Instead of accepting what they did wrong and working with us to change the situation, the guy may blame you for the failure of the relationship. You do not need that, especially when you are really trying to make things work by figuring out what is wrong. The wrong guy will never accept responsibility for what he did wrong in the relationship. A true man will, but not a man that always feels like he is right. Do not blame him for what you did wrong in the relationship. You have to take responsibility for that. But there were some things that he did wrong too that he must take accountability for.

In every relationship, it takes two people to make things work. You were not alone in the relationship so if he says that it is your entire fault, do not listen. Tell someone else how you feel to get it out or let it go. And once you have spoken about what is bothering you, find a way that helps you cope with it in a positive way like writing in a journal, walking, exercising, listening to music, watching inspirational channels, reading, or playing word or video games. You may not want to pay a psychiatrist. But at least talk to a friend that you can trust and who will not spread your secrets to other people. Talk it out so that you can release the pain and begin your journey to healing.

10. Learn to evaluate the situation for how it really is and not how you want it to be. It is okay to use emotions to make decisions sometimes. We are all human and one of the things that make us human is our ability to show compassion toward others. Never lose that because compassion is what's going to help you through life. At the same time, using your emotions to make every decision is not good. Sometimes you really have to put your emotions aside to be able to see the situation clearly. You're hoping that things will change for the better but they never do. You see the signs, but at the same time you refuse to see them. Then when you get hurt, you say to yourself that you should have gone with your mind instead of relying on your heart.

11. Don't buy his love anymore. Even if you did not spend money, do not use your time either to buy his love. You do not have to buy a man's love if he freely gives it to you. It may seem like your trying to do things for him to show him how much you care but men do not think the same way that women do. He may feel like you gave him something that he did not need or did not ask for. So it may feel like betrayal and ungratefulness to you but to

him it may seem like you were trying to buy his affection when you should have been letting him get to know you instead. He would just think, "Wow, I can get her to do anything I want her to." A man that cares for you will not make you prove your love to him. Instead, he will actually prove his love for you and will want to do things for you. Keeping up your relationship will not be stressful and you will not feel like you are the only one giving. What is your man doing to prove his affection for you? If he is not doing anything then that should help you move on faster.

12. Don't be desperate anymore. Pick the kind of guy that you want to be with. Don't change another man and try to transform him. If you order a burger at a restaurant and you tell them to put ketchup and mustard on it and they come back with onions and tomato, would you just eat the burger or would you send it back?

You send the burger back because that is not want you wanted. You may feel that you cannot fully enjoy your food because it is not what you asked for. You may feel upset that they restaurant even had the gall to try to tell you what you wanted. You do not want anyone to force you to choose something else when you know what you want. Why should your choice of a man be any different?

Men have mastered this concept. They know what type of woman they want. And when a man truly wants to get married, he looks for certain traits that he feels should be in his future wife. If a woman does not have the traits he looking for, then he sends that burger back because that is not what he wants and that is not what he ordered.

You may not have done that in the past but you can start now. The way to maintain and get a successful relationship is to look for certain traits in the man you want to be with. If you want a man to be faithful to you then do not get a pretty boy that women are always after. Do not get a player that only wants sex. Do not stay with a man that doesn't know how to treat women. Get a man that believes in being faithful to one woman. Get a man that knows how to treat a woman and pays for meals. That is the key to having a successful relationship. You have to look for traits in a guy that will guarantee a good relationship. If you are incompatible with a guy and always settling then you are going to be unhappy in your relationship.

13. Don't rely on any man to save your thinking about men as a whole. You are setting yourself up for failure. This man may be a dog from the get-go. You have just based your whole idea of men on one miserable, sorry man. No matter how bad the relationship ended or how bad your experiences were, just know that there is a good guy out there. You have been through a lot of bad men so you know what to avoid and you know to pick the opposite of what you had. But what keeps women stuck in the old relationship is that they believe that there is nothing better out there. Once you believe that, then you set yourself up to stop looking and just settle for what you had. It may take some time but he will come. It's hard to be patient, but you want to be happy with a man that cares for you. You do not know when love will come, but you have to be ready.

14. Don't grab the chocolate when you get sad. It's okay to indulge sometimes, but don't overeat. You do not have to be a size zero to be sexy and feel good about yourself. But I have never heard a woman say that she feels good when she eats a pound of cake. Keep yourself up and exercise. When you feel good, you are at your best. It is not hard to move on because you do not feel like your guy—even if he is wrong for you—is the only one that can love you. Once you start to get attention from other guys, you begin to realize that other men see something in you. If that

loser does not see anything in you then maybe he needs to get his eyes checked because other men's eyes are working just fine.

15. Don't get over emotional. Do not let a lot of things upset you. If the guy forgets your birthday, be cool. If you yell and go off at him, then he will get upset and say you always get upset. The best way to let him know that it bothered you is to wait for when his birthday comes around. Forget his a little. Maybe you want to act like you forgot. You may go on pretending all day, and then at night, call him and say, "Happy birthday. I almost forgot, but I didn't." I bet he will not forget your birthday anymore.

　　　If a guy is late for a date, stay cool; next time, just be late for something that he really wants to do. He will get there early next time because he knows how it feels to have to wait. It may sound mean but what I am saying is true. A person never knows how you feel about things until it happens to them. You can tell a person your feelings all day long, but they do not understand until it happens to them. You don't have to be mean or take it to the extreme. Just step back and show them how you are feeling rather than telling him all the time. There is nothing wrong with expressing how you feel but if he just looks like he does not care then you may just have to show him instead. Not getting emotional over a lot of things saves you from being upset and then blowing up. When you blow up, then the guy can be excused for what he did. He will turn the limelight off him and make it seem like it was your fault. He will make you feel guilty and then you will feel as if he really did not do anything wrong and that you just always get upset about nothing. So calming down and expressing your feelings calmly will keep the focus on what he's done. He will have to be accountable and it will be easier for you to move on. The wrong man will play with your emotions and pull your strings like a puppet to get you to react the way they want so that things work in their favor. Do not give your man this much power. Take it back.

16. Don't tell too much. When you tell too much, it is hard to leave because you feel so invested in the relationship. You feel like this man knows all of your secrets and he knows you, when really, he just knows how to manipulate you. I bet you if you ask him what your favorite color is he will not be able to tell you. That's okay right? You feel like he may have just forgotten, so you ask something else, like what your favorite food is. You may have even told him this detail several times so he should know. You may have eaten there last week. Do not be surprised if he does not know. You may ask him several more questions and you'll be surprised that he doesn't really know you. Now ask him what makes you mad, what your biggest pet peeve is, and what you do when you get sad. I bet he will be able to tell you without even hesitating. He probably cannot wait until you finish the question so that he can talk. And he may even give overly elaborative answers. But remember, knowing you and knowing how to manipulate you are two different things.

Feel good about yourself and you lessen his power to control your worth with manipulation. Don't give one man that much power and do not let him know everything about you. Because the wrong man will use that information against you and make you feel like you are crazy because he knows how to pull your strings and make you act like that. The less you give a man, the better off you will be. Of course, let him get to know you, but only after some time and after he has earned your trust. People put up a good game and time is the only thing that can bring that game to the light. It is only for so long that a man can keep a false front up before his real personality comes out. But if you let him come into your heart and your mind too fast then you do not see him for who he is until you're in love with him. Every time you want to leave you never can because you feel like love brings you back. So be very careful and remember to just be happy first with yourself and by yourself until you can find the right one to share your life with.

WHAT TIME IS GOOD FOR

You know the old saying "Time heals all wounds." Well that is not necessarily true. Maybe time does heal physical wounds but it does not absolutely heal emotional ones. People can grow old and still be bitter. Friends can fall out over something so simple and never speak to each other again. A woman can get hurt from one relationship and never marry. So time does not heal all wounds. The purpose of time is to give us time to heal and consciously move on. Healing has to be a conscious choice. It cannot take place unless you allow it to. It is not easy. But you have to make a conscious choice every day not to pick up your hurt but pick up hope instead. Do not keep your heart from ever loving again. Give your heart life again. Mentally dig your heart out of the pain that it is buried in. It's easy to keep our hearts bandaged after we have been wounded. The truth is muscles need to be stretched or they become stiff. The heart is the same way. Everyone wants to feel and experience love and affection. When we do not get that feeling, it is easy to harden our hearts and become bitter. Don't become bitter no matter what you have been through. Its okay go through bitterness for a season but to keep it for a lifetime is a repeated robbery. Don't allow anyone to steal your hopes or your dreams from you. Keep going on with life. Life is constantly moving even if you are not. We have all felt anger, hurt, pain, sadness, or depression at one time or another. The key to moving on from these feelings is in the moving on part. You have to keep moving so that you don't stay trapped in the same emotion. Happiness may be a mile down the road. If you never move in that direction, then you risk staying where you are. No matter how bad you may feel, keep moving. Keep this inspiring quote by author Anais Nin in mind: "And the day came when the risk to remain tight in a bud was more painful than the risk it took to blossom."

DON'T BE IMPRISONED BY YOUR PITY

It's easy to fall into the trap of staying with a man because you feel sorry for him. This kind of relationship never works. What usually happens is both parties are miserable. The relationship is built on guilt. The woman stays because she feels that it is her responsibility to save her man from his own misery. The man feels that it is her responsibly to save him. In reality, he has to save himself first.

There is nothing wrong with being there for someone in a tough time. What makes it wrong is when you do it out of guilt. You feel obligated to be there instead of wanting to be in his life. This causes stress and bitterness in the relationship. The woman feels that the man is draining all of her energy. She is doing everything to help him and he is not helping himself. The man is also angry because in his mind, the woman will never be able to do enough to heal his scars. She becomes the scapegoat, someone he can blame for not being able to solve the issues he is dealing with internally.

Every relationship goes through its trials. There are going to be times when one of you needs to lean on the other. But one person cannot carry the relationship by their lone self. Have you ever asked your girlfriends the question, "Why do you stay with him? You are so unhappy now. What hold does he have on you? Why can't you leave?" This question is common in many relationships today.

Patti is an example of a woman caught in a guilt relationship. She was thirty-one and had one child by her ex-husband and was now dating a man named Darrell. Darrell was physically abused by his alcoholic father when he was a child. He saw his father beat his mother and other brothers many times. He ran away from home when he was sixteen and joined a gang. After many years, Darrell eventually broke from the gang life by faking his own death. He later moved to Colorado where he met Patti. He never had much of a childhood or a family life. He wanted to be in a relationship that gave him that chance. Patti wanted her child to really like Darrell. Every since she and his father split, he had been sad lately. Patti knew about Darrell's past. She felt like Darrell needed her to be there for him at that time. She also wanted to give her son a male role model to help him cope with the divorce.

As months went by, Patti began to see that Darrell was constantly upset. When he spent time with her son, he was very loving and caring. The next minute he was on a rampage about something as simple as leaving a cup on the table. Patti knew Darrell was dealing with past issues that were still troubling him. So she tried to make the best of the situation by being there for him.

Darrell became worse and worse. He would get into violent rages where he would always break things. Patti and her son were walking on egg shells trying not to say anything that might upset him. One day, she forgot to pick up his favorite milk and he hit her. That was all that Patti could take. She understood that Darrell's past life was the cause of his present unhappiness, but she could not take the relationship anymore. She began to lose weight. She also noticed her son was becoming violent and aggressive toward his peers.

When Patti told Darrell the relationship was over, he cried. He begged her many times to take him back. He left flowers, numerous messages, and even drove past her house every day.

Darrell confided in Patti that she had helped to turn his life around. She did not want to get back with Darrell again, but she felt like she could help him. Reluctantly, Patti began to see Darrell again. He did try to keep his temper under control for a while. Then he began to hit Patti again. This time, he would hit her a couple times a week. Patti was miserable. She had been in an unsuccessful marriage, and now she was in an abusive relationship. She wanted a male figure in her son's life but she could not expose him to Darrell's violent rages anymore. She left a note for Darrell that said:

> It is over. Please seek counseling. I cannot take it anymore. I love you but I love my son too much to see you make his life or mine miserable any longer.
>
> —Patti

Patti could not stay in the relationship with Darrell. She could not save him. Darrell would have to seek professional counseling to begin healing from his past. If you are with a man that needs more than you can give him, then do not feel guilty for stepping back. Do not be afraid to leave in order to gain your happiness back. If you do not, then you will have to experience their painful journey with them. Most times, bitterness and anger is sure to follow.

There are men out there that want to use women as their scapegoat in life. When things do not go right, they want to blame their circumstances on the woman not being there. They want to keep the women there with guilt so that she is unhappy and goes into depression too. These kinds of men do not want you to be happy without them. Every time the woman wants to move on, that is when they automatically want to straighten up for a couple of weeks. Then when they feel like she is feeling comfortable, they go back to their old ways again. When she threatens to leave again, he sees if she is bluffing. If he feels that she is bluffing, he does not put much effort into making things right so that she will stay. If he calls her bluff wrong and realizes she is leaving him for real, he will do whatever he feels is necessary to keep the woman in his life. He will cry. He will buy the woman gifts. He will free up his calendar to spend more time with her. He will stay on the phone all night if he has to. And he will temporarily change to keep the woman in his life for the long term. Men know if they have a good woman in their life. They know that a good woman will always be there when you need her because that is just how a good woman thinks. She believes in standing by her man and being there for him through thick and thin. These types of men will always have an excuse as to why they do not want to get married or why they should never commit to you. They don't want you but they are so selfish that they do not want anyone else having you either. These types of men always want you there when they have a problem, but when everything is going right in their life they do not have any time to spend with you, that is, until you talk about leaving. These types of men are called *Indian givers*.

Indian givers is a term for people who give you things and then want to take them back when you show any interest in them. That is the same term used to describe these men. They practically give their women reasons to want to be in another relationship where they are appreciated. Then when the women get ready to leave and maybe have a chance of actually being with men that appreciates them, that is when they realize the worth of their women that they practically gave away and want them back. It does not matter if the woman has physically and emotionally moved on with another man; these men do not want the woman to be happy in any way. So they are on their best behavior just long enough to hook the woman back in, then they go back to their old ways again.

The only way to leave a bad situation is to believe that you deserve better and that there is someone better out there for you. A lot of times, what keeps women in bad situations is the fact that they do not believe that there is anyone good out there for them. These men are very good at manipulating people because they study and observe them. Their main intent is to use people to get what they want so they will try to learn everything about them. I think that is another reason why it is also hard for women to leave. They feel like no man will ever understand them like these men do, so they stay, thinking that their men have their best interests at heart since they know them so well. They stay thinking things will get better, but they never do. Time after time, the men promise that they will change but they do not. Then they play games with their emotions and make them feel guilty for not being there for them and not putting up with their mess. They may even use the reasoning that real love does not quit or give up. So they make the women feel guilty for "fleeing" when trouble comes.

But that is not the case for these women or for yourself; you are just tired of putting up with the same mess that will never change. But your man makes it seem like he does not leave you when times get too tough. And he is right; he does not. And that is because you do not treat him wrong or try to manipulate him. You are there for him and you help him out when he needs you. I would stay too if the odds were in my favor. You put up with his mess while he gets all the perks. That is why he never wants you to leave while you feel so drained and tired.

If you are in a relationship where you are doing all of the giving and he is doing all of the taking, never feel that you are a quitter. But you have to leave before you are stuck. What happens when he finds someone that he likes more than you and he leaves? You have invested all of that sweat and tears into your relationship and now he is riding off in the sunset with another woman. You are too upset and hurt that you let yourself go and now no man is really looking at you because you have all that emotional baggage that you have to try to heal from. And the thing that keeps you stuck in your mind is the fact that you gave your all and was there for him and he left you in the end. So get out of something bad and do not be afraid to leave.

Trust me when I say that these types of men do not want you to be happy and they only think about themselves. And if the table was turned and they were the ones getting used they would leave you in a heartbeat. So please do not feel obligated to stay and endure any more mess. Being married is different. Being married symbolizes a commitment between you and your partner. You promised before God to endure the good as well as the bad times. So it is a vow that you and your partner made that you are both honoring to not run when times get hard. But when you are in just a relationship, you do not have that same kind of obligation to endure what you would in marriage. Heck, you don't even have a ring to help you remember what you may be enduring all of the pain and drama for. You may be doing everything that a wife does, but in the end if he wants to leave, he will. Any man that can use a woman and treat her badly and use her will not be merciful when it comes to leaving you for another woman. And who is to say that he has not already left you for another woman? He just has not told you yet so that you can move on to a new man. Instead, he would rather keep you as a backup plan because he knows that he can always rely on you just in case she does not come through.

Don't place yourself in any position where you give any man the power to cripple you and bring you to your knees. When you see the situation is not right, leave. Leave on your own terms so that you can be happy, rather then have him leave you after you have put in all of that work. He told you that you should endure the rough times and you did. Then when he finds someone else, he doesn't even follow his own advice. And that is a hurting thing because you thought you had something and when you really look at it, you didn't even get a ring. You stayed and helped build him up and he took more than he gave. You don't have anything but memories and even those were full of fighting and tears. You might have helped him pay off some things and you even might have spent a lot of money on him to keep him happy. In the end he will not remember that if he has no good intentions for you from the start. He is looking for a woman that can take care of him the best. Don't fight to hold on to this kind of man. Let the next one have him. You did not lose anything. Trust me!

THE DIFFERENCE BETWEEN MEMORIES AND FLASHBACKS

Memories tend to be positive experiences that you never want to forget. They bring a smile to your face no matter if they took place a long time ago. Sometimes memories can keep you going when you need a booster in life. Flashbacks, on the other hand, are different. They do not produce the same effect. You can be in a good mood and a flashback will diminish it in a matter of seconds. Flashbacks happen when we think the worse about a situation. They can be triggered by just one word, action, or image. When we control our thoughts, we have more memories and fewer flashbacks. Memories are generally seen as the "best day ever." Flashbacks seem to be categorized as the "day from hell." Flashbacks can prevent you from beginning a relationship because they discourage you from trying something new. The only way to defeat a flashback is to not give it power. They are images from the past which will keep recurring until a good memory defeats it.

Flashbacks destroy relationship and often cause misunderstandings between people. Omar and Cynthia got along well as friends, but when they decided to become a couple, that was when the problems started. Cynthia had been in relationships before where men constantly cheated on her. Omar knew that Cynthia had issues with trust, but he was really upset that she did not trust him. He was not like the men that she compared him to. Sometimes Cynthia would get upset if Omar did not respond back to her text within a period of time. He explained that he was at work and sometimes he was not able to text back right away. Cynthia had heard these excuses from the men that she dated in the past. Usually they did not respond back because they were with other women. So she began to believe that whenever a man does not text back right away, he was with another woman.

Omar was becoming more and more confused with their relationship. Sometimes he wished they could have stayed friends. He knew that it was too late now to go back to being friends. He just didn't know how much more of the relationship he could take. If Omar was late meeting Cynthia, she automatically assumed he was with another woman. If they were talking on the phone and he said he was going to bed, she assumed he wanted to call another woman. There was nothing that he could do to erase the bad memories she had from her last relationships.

Omar decided that it was time to have a talk with Cynthia. He wanted to be with her but changes needed to be made in their relationship. He decided to talk with her after they had finished watching a movie together. He thought if he made it seem like it was not a big deal, she would take it better. Omar turned off the TV after the movie was over and turned toward Cynthia.

"That was a good movie." Omar laid the remote on the coffee table.

"It was a good movie. But why are you looking at me like you want to say something?" Cynthia crossed her arms and gave Omar her full attention.

"Cynthia listen, I really like you but lately, I have been feeling like I can never do anything right in this relationship. You have been through some hurtful things with the men in your past but I am not them. If something doesn't change in this relationship I—"

"You're breaking up with me? You have found another woman and you're leaving me?" Cynthia uncrossed her arms and prepared to leave.

"No, no, no!" Omar let out a deep breath.

"I'm just tired of you comparing everything I do to the men that have hurt you. I am not them. I want you to treat me like I'm a different person from them." Omar was on his feet now as he waited for Cynthia to respond.

"I cannot believe that you invited me over here for a movie and then break up with me as soon as the movie is over. Is this your way of saying we had some good times and now it is over? Are you seeing another woman? Are you telling me you do not want to be in this relationship anymore? Just be a man and say it. Don't invite me over for some damn movie to tell me this. You know this is what men do." Cynthia broke down in tears.

"See that is what I am talking about. You constantly refer to me as 'men.' I'm starting to believe that is my name now. And who is cheating on you? How did you get that out of 'We need to talk'?" Omar plopped back down on the sofa.

"Don't turn this around on me. You're tired of putting up with me; well, I am tired of putting up with you. Do you know this is pretty much how it ended with my other relationships? They always say that we needed to talk."

"I can see why," Omar muttered under his breath.

"That's what I'm talking about. You're always saying mean things like that to me. It's like you don't even care about me. I've noticed that for a while." Cynthia folded her arms across her chest and bit her lip to try to stop the tears.

"You know what? I can't do this anymore. Nothing I do is ever good enough for you. Instead of blaming me for what other men have did to you, why don't you start looking at what you might have done wrong in those relationships."

"What are you saying? Are you saying that I caused those men to treat me that way?" Cynthia began to sob.

"I don't know." Omar got up and went to the door.

"I hate you. I hate all men. You are all the same. I knew that you would do this to me. I thought you were different but I guess not." Cynthia headed toward the door and looked Omar dead in the eyes before she slammed the door behind her.

CYNTHIA'S STORY

When Cynthia got in her car, she immediately called her sister and told her what had happened in between sobs.

"Christina, Omar broke up with me today. He invited me over to his place, and then after the movie was over, he told me… that…he did not want to be with me…anymore.

"You are kidding. What did he say? Tell me everything that happened. Don't leave out any details."

"Well, he said that it was a good movie that we were watching. He turned off the TV and said that he wanted to talk. He seemed like he was really thinking of a way to break it gently to me that he wanted to break up because I was looking at his face when he said it. I've been through this before. Anytime a man says he wants to talk and turns off the TV, then it's serious."

"How did he say it? Did he pause before he said it? Did he turn to you and then pause and say it or was it like he just wanted to talk about it?"

"It was definitely a pause before he said it, like he wanted to tell me he was seeing another woman. But it was kind of like he was debating whether to tell me or not." Cynthia sobbed loudly.

"Okay, what else happened?"

"Well, he took the longest time to say anything. Then he started talking about how tired he was of our relationship. I mean relationships are not going to be happy all the time. But you don't bail on them just because you are getting bored. So I asked him why he was breaking up with me. Then he was like, 'I'm not breaking up with you; I'm just tired of you comparing me to other men. That's my name now, men,'" Cynthia said sarcastically.

"No, he didn't. What made him say that?"

"I don't know. Maybe because he's cheating. You know that every time a man cheats, he starts downing you. Then he talks about how tired he is of being in the relationship."

"Did you catch him? Did he tell you that he was cheating?"

"No, but I can tell. It's just something about the way he said that we needed to talk. It's like he really wanted to tell me something. I don't know what brought this on. Can you believe that he tried to make it seem like it was my fault, when he was the one that was cheating on me?"

"Men!" Christina shook her head.

"Can you believe he told me I caused men to cheat on me because I complain all the time?"

Cynthia paused and waited for Christina to say something. When Christina did not say anything, she continued.

"You know what. I don't know why men do this. It's like they are scared of commitment. We never had this problem when we were friends. Now that we became a couple, it's like he doesn't want to be with me anymore. You know, I was reading a relationship book that said men hate relationships. It scares them because they feel trapped. Being with other women helps relieve the tension. The book said just to give them time and then they will come back because they no longer feel trapped anymore. I can tell you one thing; if he wants to come back, I'm not taking him back."

OMAR'S STORY

After Cynthia left, Omar thought about the situation in his head. Cynthia was acting really weird lately. He just wanted to talk, but they ended up breaking up. He really liked Cynthia, but he wasn't so sure she would ever move on from her past relationships. He decided to call his buddy Eddie to get some insight.

"Hey, man, what's up?" Eddie said

"Nothing man. Hey, you want to hear something crazy? I invited Cynthia over for a movie and we broke up." Omar laughed.

"What happened? What did you do?"

"I didn't do anything. You know how I told you that she was always comparing me to her exes? Well, I just confronted her about it today. I told her we needed to talk and make some changes in the relationship.

"Oh, dude. You should have never done that. I need to talk to a chick means we need to break up. Why did you do that? Listen man: rule number one: never ever say to a woman 'We need to talk.' Rule number two: never ever tell a chick anything is wrong with the relationship. Have I taught you nothing?" Eddie shook his head.

"I needed to talk to her because I just could not take it anymore. She even accused me of cheating on her. Then she starts crying and comparing me to other men. That aggravates the hell out of me when she does that. Eddie, come on man, tell me you would not have done the same thing?" Omar threw up his hands in frustration.

"Naw man. I'm trying to stay in my relationship. Women hate to hear that anything is wrong with the relationship. Just give her some time to cool down and buy her some roses." Eddie said.

"See, that is why I never call you." Omar laughed and shook his head.

"Hey man, I'm still in my relationship." Eddie laughed.

"Alright, man. I'll talk to you later." Omar shook his head while hanging up the phone.

Both parties felt like they had been attacked by the other person. What turned out to be a simple conversation ended up in a breakup. Flashbacks ruin relationships and keep women from enjoying happiness with a new man in their life. When Omar tried to communicate with Cynthia, she compared him to other men rather than listening. Cynthia was not wrong in voicing how she felt. But she did not give Omar a chance to voice his opinions. Omar felt unfairly treated in the relationship because he was paying for other men's mistakes. In order to have a successful relationship you have to judge a man only for his actions. Cynthia judged Omar for what other men did to her. It is hard not to relive the pain. But remember, flashbacks have no power until we give it to them. The only way they can survive is when we keep them alive in our hearts.

I HEAR YOU, BUT I'M STILL TALKING!

Omar and Cynthia thought they were communicating with each other, but actually, they were not. One was not willing to listen to the other because they both felt attacked. You should never avoid saying how you really feel in a relationship. This does not help you or the other person. Communication is effective when both people listen to the other person no matter how much you might want to defend yourself. If Cynthia had listened to Omar, she would have realized how he felt when she compared him to her exes. Cynthia probably didn't even know what she was doing. One thing that is clear is that there is a lack of communication in their relationship. Cynthia jumped from "We need to talk" to "We need to break up." Never react when you are angry. No matter how much you want to retaliate with a mean comment, hold on to those words. When you are angry, you can never take back your words once you have said them. Words have as much power as fists do. Fists leave physical marks but words leave emotional scars. Emotional wounds take just as long to heal or even longer as physical scars.

Omar did say some hurtful things that made Cynthia feel like she was being attacked. It is important that both parties sit down and have an honest discussion about their feelings. The main objective should not be to hurt each other. It should be to understand each person's point of view. Instead of saying, 'I feel' try saying, 'I know you must feel.' Try understanding your partners' point of view. You may not fully understand why they feel the way they, do but they will feel thankful to you for trying to understand.

Miscommunication comes from the way we word things when we are talking to each other. Before Omar could finish his sentence by telling Cynthia they needed to talk, she was comparing him to other men. One response Cynthia could have used to communicate her frustration was: "Omar, are you breaking up with me? Because that is what it sounds like to me. Or do you really just want to talk?" This response would have been received better by Omar. The anger and accusation in Cynthia's voice caused him to become just as angry and defensive. Omar was frustrated and no longer wanted to discuss the situation. Cynthia and Omar could not effectively communicate; therefore, they were left feeling attacked and angry.

In a relationship, do not confuse needed communication for a reason to break up. Breakups can be avoided if both parties sat down and talked out their relationship. Of course, it is up to both parties to decide if their relationship is at the breakup point. A breakup should be the last and final resort in a relationship. A couple certainly should not break up without trying to solve their differences through communication first.

Without listening to what Omar had to say, Cynthia was ready to end the relationship. She even made a comment to her sister Christina that no matter what Omar said it was over. This is called blocked communication. Omar was speaking about his feelings, but Cynthia did not want to hear it, so he immediately became defensive. When one party is upset, it is best to limit communication or not communicate at all until both parties can respond in a receptive and calm manner.

Cynthia was not wrong in feeling the way that she did. Cynthia just expressed her feelings in an aggressive manner to Omar. She should not have begun a new relationship until she had healed from her old ones. She blamed Omar for her last relationships because she was still hurt. She was not really blaming Omar. Rather, she was really upset with the men in her past and those feelings flowed into her current relationship. Cynthia was in a current relationship with Omar, but her heart and mind were still in "flashback" mode.

The only way to completely heal from your old relationships is to give yourself time to heal. Give your wounds time to close up before getting into another relationship with a man. If he is the right one for you, he is not going anywhere. Explain to him that you need time to deal with some issues in your life. Of course, after you have healed, you still have to make a conscious choice not to categorize all men. The good news is that healing will give you a fresh mindset that will enable you to separate the new man in your life from the old ones.

MOTIVATION, WHERE ARE YOU?

Don't read romance books all day if you feel lonely. These books add to your loneliness, especially right after a breakup. There is nothing wrong with reading romance books, but if you are getting depressed, then pick up another book. Instead, try to read uplifting books that encourage you to celebrate life or find happiness doing positive things. Try to stay away from romantic movies when you have just experienced a breakup or are feeling lonely. All these movies do is depress women who do not have a man. Again, there is nothing wrong with a romantic movie. But if you are on your third bowl of ice cream, then you might want to pop in some motivational DVDs instead.

Motivational tapes are not lame. They are actually inspiring. What they do is help you train your mind to think about positive thoughts. It's not hard to focus on how lonely you are and start to have a pity party for yourself. What a motivational tape, CD or DVD does is help you move on. They help you move out of the negative realm of thinking into a more positive one.

What happens when you think of all the bad relationships you have been in? You start to feel sluggish. You feel angry and you feel like all men are the scum of the earth. Then you don't feel like doing much of anything. It drains your energy until you are sleepy and tired. Try to keep yourself encouraged. Give yourself a boost even when your heart feels like it just wants to hide. You'll be surprised at how just redirecting your thoughts can bring about a change in your life. It will not be easy, but at least you are reaching out for hope. And pretty soon, you will be able to grab it again.

This is very important. What happens when you are lonely and you are supposed to be in a relationship? Some women experience deeper depression when they are in the wrong relationship than when they were single. If a bad relationship is making you eat, cry, and stay in the bed all day, then you need to let that baggage go. You have to ask yourself if staying in a bad relationship is worth the emotional stress that is it causing you. If the positives of the relationship do not outweigh the negative emotional stress of the relationship, then you need to let things go.

Staying positive and getting all the negativity out your life is not just limited to words and thoughts, but actually also relates to healthy living. A lot of times, women will stay in bad relationships because they figure nothing better will come along and any man is better than no man. They really would like to get out of the situation they are in, but when they go on dates or look around at the dating pool, they get discouraged and they think they are better off staying with the man they have no matter how bad he may be. That is not true. Leave this man before he takes you to the point where you're fed up and are so disgusted with men that you have to take a long time to heal afterwards. There are some good men out there. The reason why it's hard to find these good men is that women will not let the bad ones go. We go through so much with the bad ones that when a good man comes along, we have nothing left for him. Do not be afraid to be by yourself until you find a good man. Remember you can say there are no good men left, but you cannot blame a man for treating you bad when you're the one that would not let go even when he showed you who he was.

THE GRASS IS NOT ALWAYS GREENER ELSEWHERE

The grass isn't greener on the other side. Sometimes we look in other people's "yards" too much and compare it to our own that we don't see the good things we have going on. Never look at someone else's relationship and compare it to your own. You will be surprised at how this comparison makes you feel bad about your own relationship. Every relationship is going to be different because everybody's personalities are different. Never compare yourself to another woman. Do not feel bad because you are different. A woman that is not afraid to be herself offers variety and excitement in the dating world. What if everyone talked the same or ate all the same foods? The world would be a boring place. You could predict other's people's actions because they are the same as yours.

There is something special about you that cannot be duplicated by any other woman in the world. A lot of women are trading in this uniqueness to become acceptable in men's eyes. The only problem is beauty is in the eyes of the beholder. Do not hide behind a mask that is not you. Take the mask off and be proud of who you are. The only thing about a mask is you can become afraid to take it off. Acceptance is when a man likes you despite of what you might believe to be your flaws. Hiding behind a mask actually tricks men; you cheat them out of knowing the real you. Eventually the real you will come out. Then you have to go through the pain of feeling like you have betrayed yourself and those around you.

Do not be ashamed to show men your real personality. If someone is going to accept you, there is nothing that you can do to change their opinion. Just go on and be happy with your life. He is just one man and he does not stop the world from moving. Changing does not help him like you if he chooses not to.

In life, there are some men that will accept you and there are others that will reject you. You just have to find that person. Do not spend half of your life trying to convince one man of all the reasons he should like you. One man just isn't worth that much energy or stress. I do agree that being rejected is an awful feeling. When you are rejected, remember that everybody does not have the same taste. They are not supposed to. Variety makes the world go round, so thank God for it.

Beauty is skin-deep. So every man's idea of beauty is going to be different. It's really about finding a guy that connects with you rather than changing yourself to fit another man's preference.

So what if one man or even four men did not like about you? Another man will. A saying goes, "One man's junk is another man's treasure"; what one man considers trash could be gold to another man.

Do not base your self-esteem on how one man looks at you. His opinion does not reflect all men's opinion of you. Most importantly, believe in your own heart that you are beautiful. You are a beautiful person that deserves to give this beauty to the right man.

DIFFERENT ISN'T ALWAYS BAD

Taking time to know yourself also means taking time to be ready to be with someone else. A lot of times, hurting women will expect their men to read their mind. They want their guys to know them better than they know their own selves. I can tell you from experience that this is not going to work. You must know and learn to love yourself first. And even if the man tries really hard to love you, it's hard to let someone love you when you haven't even learned to love yourself first.

Every time a man wants to get close to you, you push him away because you do not feel like you are worthy of his love. Then when he gets tired of trying to break down your walls and stops, he will eventually approach another woman that doesn't have the same issues you do. What attracts men to women is they see a confidence that attracts their attention. Confidence in a woman tells the guy she is not afraid to be herself and that she likes who she is. He can be in a room with a hundred women, but his eyes will always be drawn to the woman who is sure of herself. I am in no way saying that you have to be perfect or the prettiest woman in the room. But you do have to love yourself for who you are before you can ask anyone else to.

I think that most women develop low self-esteem from childhood teasing or a father that was not there. Or maybe they had a father that constantly compared them to others or often expressed his disapproval of them. Some women have even been sexually or emotionally abused by the men in their lives. The issues that often stem from these experiences stop them from being able to accept a man who truly loves them. No matter what reason you have for having low self-esteem, know that you are worthy of love. You do not have to be pretty to have value. You do not have to have a ton of money to have value. It does not matter what kind of car you drive or what kind of job you have; you have value. You are worthy of being loved. There is someone out there for everyone. You just have to wait for the right person to come along and recognize that truly special gem that is shining inside of you.

Show a man that you have something to offer him that is unique and different from other women. Show him the uniqueness that can be found in your mind and in your heart. A woman's beauty is defined not just by her curves but also by her heart. Her personality gives her beauty. A woman does not need a man to define who she is or who she should be. A woman is a piece of art because she has many different qualities that make up her identity. Don't give a man a limited view of yourself. Let him see you with his eyes and his heart.

HAVE I GOT GAME FOR YOU!

The worst thing a woman can do is play games to get a man. I have read some books that teach women games that guarantee them the attention of a man. The way you start with a man is the way you have to finish. If you play games in the beginning, you will be playing games for the rest of the relationship. Games and psychology do work. But the downside of the game is that you can never stop because that is what hooked the man in the first place. So if you start to feel like you love him and want to stop, don't be surprised if he doesn't feel for you like he did at first.

Then you want to throw the rules away and start being yourself and he acts like he does not want to spend time with you. You get upset because you're falling for him and he doesn't seem to be falling for you now that you're trying to be yourself. So you blame men and rules. You want to get upset with men and use this experience as an excuse to have to play games with men because they do not respond to anything else. Then when you do find a good man, you treat him wrong because you're mad at the other men in your past. He gets hurt and then he goes out and hurts other women because he tried to be a good man and he feels women don't really want a good man.

So a word of caution to women before they play games: just be yourself. There's nothing wrong with having morals and taking things slow. The only thing about games is they only excite men for a short time. Then they are ready to move on to someone else after the fun is over. There has to be something different about you from the other women he has dated. The only way you can be different is just to be yourself. Let him like you for who you are. And if he cannot accept you for you, don't lose your real self trying to be want he wants you to be.

You can play games with people's heads but games do not fool the heart. When someone really cares about you, you do not have to play games. Treat other people the way you want to be treated. If you do not want someone playing games with you, then don't do the same to his heart. Playing games will not make a man magically care for you. Let a man fall for you through your qualities and not through the games you play.

Learn from the story of Maria and Carlos. Maria was a woman that believed in pleasing her man at all costs. Carlos liked Maria because she was different from most women. She was not afraid to take chances. She was adventurous, and she was not afraid to try anything at least once. Maria was attracted to Carlos because he was so composed even in the most stressful situations. He was grounded and knew what he wanted to do in life. She felt like

Carlos would be the kind of man that wouldn't let anything get in the way of his dreams.

Maria knew Carlos liked the wild side of her because she would do things that he was too scared to do. So Maria started to really get into clubbing and drinking. She would bring Carlos along and show him how to have a good time. He seemed to really have fun. He liked it when Maria would grab the microphone at the club and start singing although she could not sing. He liked how confident she was and how she was not scared of what anyone thought of her. Sometimes she would get up and start dancing in front of everyone. She would not stop until she had the attention of everyone in the club. Carlos tried to hide it, but he liked that side of Maria.

Soon Maria began to drink a lot to loosen up more. Carlos seemed to like that side of her so she wanted to keep up what was working. The problems started when Maria could not control her drinking. She started to drink in the morning, all through the evening, and before she went to bed. Sometimes Maria would be so drunk from the night before that she would find different men and women in her bed. She started to feel out of control but she could not stop herself. She felt incredible guilt when she could not remember what she did on the nights she became really drunk, but in order to deal with the guilt she drunk even more.

Carlos was beginning to not want Maria anymore. He liked Maria in the beginning because she was not afraid to take risks, and she was the kind of person that he felt was a free spirit. But lately, he felt Maria had become too much of a free spirit. He just could not deal with that type of woman. Carlos liked to drink and have a good time too, but the Maria he fell in love with was one that was now out of control.

When Carlos broke it off with Maria, she was hurt. He had always told her that he liked that side of her that was not afraid to be herself and to let go. And now he was breaking up with her because of that very reason. It hurt Maria when Carlos left, but she wanted to show him that he made a big mistake. So she began to party and drink more often. Months later, she found out Carlos had begun dating. Her friends had seen him with his new girl. She never saw Carlos go to the clubs or to parties with this new girl. She knew the relationship would not last long. This new girl was just a rebound for him. He would get bored with her and come back to Maria, begging her to take him back. Months went on and Maria could see how serious he was becoming about this new woman in his life.

Maria could not understand it. This new girl was completely the opposite of her. She was more serious and she really did not know how to have fun, but Carlos seemed to be in love with her. Maria was miserable; she had been fired from her job for being tardy too many times, and she was having trouble finding a new one. She could not keep a boyfriend, and on top of everything, she was pregnant and wasn't sure who the father was. Maria became bitter. Men did not know what they wanted. She felt like men used women to get what they wanted and then they move on to the next one. She sacrificed so much for Carlos. She was there for him when he needed her. She was cool and proved she knew how to have a good time. She drunk because he liked it at first then he broke up with her because of it. She didn't even drink that much before she met him. Now he was with a girl that did not even drink. Maria went into a depression when she learned that after eight months he was planning on getting married to the new woman in his life. They had been together for three years and he never once mentioned marriage. Whenever she brought up the subject, he always brushed it off or changed the subject.

Maria was not a bad person. She just changed into the person she thought Carlos wanted. In the process, she lost who she was by trying to be what she thought would make Carlos stay. Be yourself, because whether he stays or goes, at least in the end you will not feel like you sacrificed who you were.

GOT COMPATIBILITY?

Compatibility is very important in a relationship. It is true that opposites attract, but even among opposites, there must be some compatibility. There must be a common ground that you can both connect on. When a man and a woman are completely different and cannot find anything in common, this can become a cause for the breakup of their relationship. They start getting into arguments all the time. Sometimes just choosing a place to eat out can lead to drama.

Mike and Tiffany were two people who had met at an art exhibit. They hit it off and eventually dated. They were different ages. Mike was twenty-nine and Tiffany was twenty-four. Both were very different but this was what attracted them to each other. Because they were such opposites, they found each other to be exciting. They spent hours on the phone talking about their different experiences and life philosophies. Although they never quite agreed with one another, they decided to support and accept their differences.

Eventually, things began to get serious between the two and they started to talk about the future. Mike wanted to have children, but Tiffany was not ready yet. She knew that she wanted to have children one day, but at that time she wanted to focus on her career. Tiffany was very religious and Mike was not. He believed there was a God out there somewhere but he wasn't particularly looking for him. If Tiffany did get married, she wanted their children to be Baptist, and Mike thought their children should be free to choose their own religion.

Tiffany loved exotic foods and traveling. She wanted to travel the world and see new places one day. As soon as she had saved up enough money, she wanted to pursue her passion and live in Rome for a year. Mike was more stationary and reserved in trying new things. He wanted to continue working in the bookstore where he was currently employed.

Mike liked to listen to mellow music with a rhythm and blues flow. Tiffany liked country and pop/rock. She was always encouraging him to come to a concert with her but he preferred small entertainment settings to crowded ones.

Mike liked adventure and science fiction movies while Tiffany liked romance and dramatic films. He would try to get her to go to the cinema with him, but they never could agree on the movies they wanted to see. Usually they ended up not going to the movies or staying at home watching cable.

Tiffany was not a big organizer. Mike, on the other hand, liked to have everything in a particular place or it would drive him nuts. They would constantly argue over minor details such as putting a cup on a coaster or putting the dishes up after they were washed. Tiffany didn't see these minor details as important, but to Mike they were very aggravating.

Every time Mike and Tiffany would try to sit down and have a conversation it would end in a big argument. They could not find anything that they had in common. At first, it was a thrill in the relationship that they were so different. Then it just became a major annoyance to each other. They could never decide on a movie. It would take hours just to find a restaurant they both liked to eat at. Tiffany wanted to do more things in life, but Mike was comfortable with being more settled and one day raising a family.

Tiffany began to get depressed in the relationship. She was not happy, and often times, she wished she was anywhere else than with Mike. No matter how much time they spent with each other, Tiffany found it sickening. Eventually they split up after a year and a half.

Opposites do attract, but there must be a middle ground that you both agree on. Everyone is different. Everyone thinks differently and has different personalities. What causes the most problems in relationships is when both people are too different that they never can agree on anything. There is not a common bond in anything to help them spend more time together. Instead, they disagree on everything because they are too opposite in their ideas, beliefs, interests, and personalities. It's good to be different and think differently, as long as there are some things that you both have in common and can agree on.

SAVE THE FIGHT

There are going to be so many things that you can fight about in a relationship. Sometimes you don't even have to try to look for something to fight about—it just happens. There are some things in a relationship you may have to overlook if you want to have a long lasting relationship. I'm not saying to overlook crucial things in the relationship. I'm only talking about minor arguments. For example, your guy sets his cup down without a saucer. Instead of arguing because he never sets the cup on a saucer, you can quietly go get a saucer and set the cup on it. I'm not saying that you can never express your feelings. What I am saying is some things are not worth fighting about. If your partner were to end up in the hospital, would the saucer stains even matter? I think we would gladly overlook saucer stains if a human life is at risk. Save the fights for the bigger things in life like cheating, abuse, or theft.

There are going to be a lot of things in life that you can fight about. So don't get discouraged and start thinking you have missed your chance. A lot of relationships break up over the small, insignificant things in life. Life is just too short to spend all of your time fighting. Instead, try to create a harmonious and joyful relationship with laughter and love. You will find out that if you create a relationship full of trust, laughter, and love then everything else will fall into place in your relationship.

With that said, it is unrealistic to think that you and your partner will never have another argument or misunderstanding. That is not true. What is true is that you can condense the amount of arguments in your relationship by choosing to enjoy a love that is forgiving towards one another and which allows for mistakes and imperfection. One common misconception is the idea that the man for you will be perfect. He will never say one thing to hurt your feelings. He can see into your heart and read your thoughts. He will smother you with love and whisk you away to a romantic island every weekend. He will be so sweet and perfect. All I have to say is that this type of man just does not exist. The media will have you to believe that he does and he is out there. But what I am saying is that love sees and it also has a blind side. In love, you should try to see the good qualities in a person that make them special and beautiful.

The same things apply to men. They see our physical traits with their eyes. Then they should be able to close their eyes and see our souls not attached to our physical beauty. They should see the part of our hearts and minds that truly makes us beautiful. Just because someone looks very good on the outside doesn't mean that the inside is necessarily the same way. It's kind of like cooking. We all know from experience that chicken can look so brown and golden on the outside; that is, until you poke your fork through it. Everyone knows when a chicken is still bleeding you have to put it back in the stove. Well, some men are the same way. They may appear perfect on the outside but they could be the most terrible, inconsiderate, and vainest men you will ever meet. Some men are so into themselves that they do not know how to talk to or treat women.

I'm not telling you to lower your standards. But how many great men have you passed up because he was not Superman? Do not get caught up in superficial looks. If you find a guy that looks great and has a great personality then keep him. There is certainly nothing wrong with having the whole package. But never stay with a man that treats you wrong just because the outside package is wrapped pretty. I can assure you if you ever opened up the package, you wouldn't be pleased by what's inside.

THE MORALS IN A MAN

Morals matter in life because they tell us what is right and what is wrong. One thing you should look for in a man is morals. Never talk to a man who talks down to women. When a man respects you, he will talk like it. If you are talking to a man and all he does is talk about sex, then leave him alone. Any real man that respects you will have more to talk about than sex. A real man does not curse around you. Cursing is a sign of disrespect and anger. When a man can cuss right in front of you then he does not mean you any good. The English language is designed with so many words that allow a person to express themselves in a respectable and intelligent manner. There is no reason why a man should feel that he has to curse in front of a woman to get his point across.

If you are talking to a man that already has a girlfriend then leave him alone. For one thing, if he can cheat on her then he can cheat on you. Please do not fall into the trap of thinking he might do it to her but he won't do it to you. Please do not fall into the trap of thinking that it is love. If it were love then he would have broken up with her and then dated you. The fact that he is still with her means that he may be bored or just want you for sex. A good man will not do this. A man will only do what you allow him to do in a relationship. If he thinks that you are okay with him talking to other women then that is what he is going to do. You want to let a man know in the beginning of a relationship what you will and will not take. You do not have to sit down and go over a list. Let him know what you will or will not take by being firm in your actions.

COMPROMISE AND RUBBER BANDS

A lot of relationships break up because no one is willing to compromise in the relationship. A good relationship does not have two dominators. Have you ever seen two people try to go in the same door at the same time? Neither one ends up getting into the door because they both have a desire to be the first ones in. It's only when someone in the relationship bends that they are both able to go inside the door. In a relationship, there must be some bending on each end to make the relationship work. No one likes to be dominated or forced to do anything.

Compromise is misinterpreted at times. It is often considered a sign of weakness but it actually takes a lot of strength. Think about it this way. Anyone can say, "No, I'm not bending. You bend." It takes a very strong person to say, "You know what, I'll bend." Pride is what really helps to destroy most relationships. One person thinks if they give in then the other person will take advantage of them. That is certainly not the case. If both people are not willing to bend then the relationship becomes stiff and stifled. No one is willing to bend so the relationship stays in one place and doesn't go anywhere. A relationship is like a rubber band.

What happens to a rubber band that is never used? It just sits there. What happens when you pick the rubber band up and began to use it? It changes form. It begins to stretch and serve a purpose. Sometimes we think if we stretch too much then we will break. The effect is just the opposite. When rubber bands are stretched, they hold things together. Flexibility in a relationship can actually hold two people together, because both people feel the relationship is held together not by manipulation but by free will.

Relationships are oftentimes guided by rules which are simply a form of manipulation to a certain degree. The rules are in place to influence how the other person should feel. For example, as a woman, you may have been taught to play hard to get in the beginning of a relationship. Even if you are very interested in a guy, you should never let on. The psychology of the game is this behavior makes him want you even more. What happens when men stretch and say "I really like you"? The woman opens up and says "You know what I really like you too." Then what would really be the purpose of rules or manipulation? If both are willing to bend a little then their relationship can go to the next level. No one has to be scared of seeming weak to the other person.

Sometimes we allow rules to guide us instead of our hearts. Rules hinder our growth in relationships because we cannot be ourselves. Rules help us to get into other people's mind and manipulate their actions. When we lose the rules, we allow the other person to do things out of their own free will. They are able to show you that they love you on their own accord, instead of being manipulated into doing so.

Let's look at Katie and Justin's relationship. Justin was a guy that always felt that if a girl liked him then she would have to prove it to him. Katie was always the kind of woman that believed love and respect should be earned not given. She had been reading relationship books since the age of fifteen. She was twenty-two and practically knew every relationship rule in the book. Justin, on the other hand, believed he wrote the book on romance. He didn't want to waste time reading things that he already knew about. Justin was twenty-six when he met Katie. What attracted the two to each other was the fact they wanted to break the other one down. In the very beginning of their relationship, they felt very bored with each other. They could never decide to do anything because the other person would always disagree with the idea. Whenever they talked on the phone, the conversation would always end in an argument. Neither one could let the other have the last word. If Katie made a comment then Justin would make a sarcastic remark. If he made a comment, she would pay him back for the previous sarcastic comment he had made towards her.

When Katie and Justin went out on dates, they were always in competition with one another. The other hated to seem weak or inferior to the other. If Katie won then the date was over. If Justin won, he rubbed it in Katie's face the whole night until she would tell him to take her home. If they went on double dates, they always got a long better with their friends' date than with each other. Justin and Katie's family could not believe that they had stayed together for almost a year. They were both constantly fighting and arguing that strangers thought they were brother and sister.

Finally, after two years, both agreed to just be friends. They were bored with each other because neither one could break the other down. After a while, Katie and Justin eventually dated other people and stopped communicating. During this time, they both fell in and out of love. They both matured in the different relationships that they experienced. One day at a local college football game, Katie and Justin met again. She was twenty-seven and Justin was thirty-one. When they saw each other, feelings sparked again between them. Both decided it would be too awkward to get into a relationship but that they should stay close friends. This time when they both went out on dates, they decided they just wanted to have fun. Katie and Justin had more fun because they were open to each other's suggestions. If they talked on the phone, they were silly and open with each other, and weren't afraid to talk about their feelings or let the other one bring up new topics and suggestions. Sometimes they would stay on the phone for hours before they realized they were going to have a high cell phone bill.

As Katie and Justin were talking one day, they noticed that they were more compatible as friends than they ever were in a relationship.

"Hey, Kat, don't you think it's strange that we get along better as friends then we ever did as a couple?" Justin laughed.

"I know. It's so weird…how big your head has gotten over the years." Katie poked Justin's head like it would pop.

"Kate. Stop playing. My head is perfect just like it always has been." Justin pouted.

"I guess. Now that you mention it, I think it's always been that big." Katie laughed. Justin shot her a look that said the jokes were over.

"Yeah, I guess I've noticed that too. I mean, how we get along better now as friends. I guess wine and friends are the same. It's better with age."

Katie shrugged. They walked in silence for a long time before he spoke again.

"I don't know about you but I've changed in the last three years. I used to think that a relationship was a game. You couldn't let the other person see you sweat. But now, I'm not so sure I feel that way anymore." Justin stopped walking and looked at Katie.

"I used to think relationships were like chess. You had to outsmart the other person to win the game. Now I believe that relationships are the total opposite. Sometimes you have to close your eyes to win…" Katie paused and she looked into Justin's eyes.

"To let your heart see for you."

Katie and Justin were two people who had believed that stretching meant a sign of weakness. Stretching can be fun if it is done right. Stretching relaxes muscles from tension that would build unless they were stretched. Look at the effects that stretching has on the physical body. If we did not stretch, imagine how stiff our muscles would be. A good relationship also needs to be stretched so that it does not become stiff.

HAVE YOU SEEN MY HUSBAND?

Every man you meet will not be your husband. Men have mastered this mentality. They do not think every woman they meet is their potential wife. In fact, most men look at most of their relationships as experiences they can learn from before they finally give their heart to the woman they'll marry. Men do not fall in love as much or as often as women do. The average woman on the other hand is completely different. Most women do fall hard for most of the men that they date. There's nothing wrong with caring for a person or wanting to treat them right. But remember, you need to relax while you're waiting for Mr. Right. When he comes you will know it.

Most women try to search for their future husband and get discouraged when they find the wrong men instead. There is nothing wrong with keeping your eyes open. Just don't stress yourself out trying to look for him at a basketball game with nine-inch heels on. Don't dress up to go check your mailbox. Don't go to random places searching for men that might be your next husband. Trust me, when a man is interested in you then he does the searching and initiating. I'm not saying you shouldn't dress up for yourself. But don't be afraid to live life because you think you have to dedicate every moment to finding a man.

Love is like searching all over your room for something that you have lost. You can search the whole place seven times and not find what you are looking for. Finally you decide that you will find it when you find it. So you straighten up your room and go to bed. A week later, when you're not searching, that is when you actually find what you were looking for. You found the item when you least expected it, on the day you were not searching for it. Well love is the same way. A lot of times we think we know when love is coming. Love is not so simple to figure out. I encourage you to live your life in the meantime while you are waiting for love to come. Keep your eyes and your heart open. But don't stress yourself out waiting for its arrival.

DON'T START ANYTHING YOU CAN'T FINISH

A lot of relationships suffer because women are not really truthful with men in the beginning of their relationship. They're just happy to get a man that they might have added a little bit to the truth or told some seemingly harmless fibs. I'm not saying that you have to tell your whole life story on the first date. But you shouldn't exaggerate the truth in order to keep a man. What happens when we make fibs is that you have to keep it up. The man begins to like you for who you have portrayed yourself to be. Even if you confess the truth later on in the relationship, it comes across to him as playing games. He does not understand that you were afraid to tell him the truth. He just knows that you told an exaggerated lie and posed it as the truth.

It's better to tell the person the truth in the beginning than to have it come out in the end. If someone is going to accept you then they are going to accept you for you. When a man really likes you then there is nothing you can do to change his mind. He accepts you for who you are, even the things you believe to be your biggest flaws. Some women mess up when they say and do things to impress a man. For instance, if you know that you do not cook then don't act like you're another Betty Crocker. Be yourself; let him know that you do not cook. If you want to take some cooking classes then let it be your own choice. Do not lie because you think that will impress him. He does not know that it is a lie so he expects you to keep it up. When you don't keep it up, he may think that you changed. He may even believe you don't care about the relationship anymore. Being truthful might seem embarrassing in the beginning but it will save you a lot of tears in the end.

DRESSING TO IMPRESS

Some women dress a certain way to get a man. When they stop dressing that way, it seems like the man isn't into them anymore.

You can use the excuse that men just don't want a good woman but sometimes that is not the case. The way you dress attracts certain type of men. If you dress provocatively, then you catch men that like the provocative attire. Most of the time, this man is only looking for one thing. When he saw you in a provocative outfit, he did not think, *Wow, she looks like a really smart and kind person.* He was thinking with his eyes and lustful instincts.

The whole time he was talking to you, he was probably only staring at your body. Be very careful, once these men get what they want, they vanish. On the other hand, when you dress with your own sense of style, it seems to capture the right man's attention. Any woman can get attention in some really short shorts; it really says something when a woman can be covered up and receive the same amount of attention. I'm not saying that you have to wear turtle necks in the summer or skirts that sweep the ground. But a man that really cares about a woman does not want his woman showing all of her goods to other men. If he really doesn't care about you then he doesn't care what you dress like. A man doesn't get upset about a woman he really does not care about. When a man really cares about you then you do not have to dress provocatively in a relationship. When a man accepts you for you then you are allowed to respect yourself. You can be sexy but still dress with respect too. In a real man's mind, he cannot understand why you dress provocative if that is not you. He accepts you for you so he doesn't know why you are trying to be another person. There is nothing wrong with dressing sexy. You do not have to stress yourself out trying to dress like a Playboy bunny. There is more to a woman than just her body. A woman should be liked for her mind and heart.

When a woman dresses very provocatively, she sends the wrong message to men. She sends the message that she does not respect herself and he shouldn't either. So when a man looks at a woman dressing provocatively, he likes her for who she is portraying herself to be. If a woman stops dressing provocatively and begins to dress more conservatively then he loses interest. She is portraying herself to be someone different than the person he met in the beginning of the relationship. So in other words, dress the way that you want a man to treat you. If you want a man to treat you like he just wants sex from you then dress that way. If you want a man to treat you with respect then dress appropriately.

I'm not telling you this to make you feel bad or to preach to you. I'm telling you this because there are so many hurting women out there. I was one of them for so long that I decided to make some changes in my life. I wanted to take my past mistakes and use them to make better choices in my future. If I wanted a good man then I was going to have to change my thinking. Sometimes we can use the excuse that men just don't want a good woman; in reality, we are doing everything to attract the wrong men. With a good man, a woman does not have to play games or go over dating secrets in her head. The way to attract a good man is just to be you and be ready to receive him when he comes.

BURY THE PAIN

When relationships become too painful, our minds tend to take the less painful route. Sometimes our minds block things from our memory by using this process: deny, suppress, and divert. *Deny* that your heart is hurting from your past relationship. *Suppress* those negative feelings by acting like they are not there. *Divert* your attention by getting into a new relationship. This will allow you not to think about the old one you are still hurting from. Before you can move on, you have to deal with the past so that it has no control over your future.

The number one thing that stops a lot of women from having a successful relationship with a new man is the fact that they believe that every man is the same. Unless you have dated every man in the world then this is an untrue statement. Every man is not the same. Yes, there are some men out there that do women wrong. There are also some good men still out there that treat women with love and respect. Make a choice in your mind that you deserve to be happy with someone that loves and respects you. Life is too short to be mistreated and choose to be alone because one man did not want to love you. There are too many men out here to let one man influence your perception of all men.

Recognize the signs of men that only want to use women. Stay away from them; keep your eyes and heart open for a good man that is right for you. Good men come into our lives but we cannot see them because we are still hurting from bad men that have stolen our hearts. Do not put a mental sign on your forehead that says Doormat or Still Hurting. Put a sign on it that says "Respect me, love me, and care for me." When the right man comes he will know; he is the right man to love a real woman.

Every woman is different therefore every woman is going to react differently to the pain that she has experienced. Don't look at other women's healing process. Find your own healing process that works for you. Don't feel bad because you could not heal the same way another woman did. Look in your own heart and try things that help you heal in your own time. Let's look at some different ways to take the pain and replace it with happiness and healing.

KEEP YOUR HEART READY

What stops a woman from being with a good man is the fact that she is not mentally ready when he comes. If a woman has encountered all the wrong men then she needs some time to prepare for a good man's arrival. It can seem like this knowledge should come naturally but the truth is that everybody has to be taught how to love each other. When you were a child, you were taught to have manners and how to treat others well. You were taught the difference between right and wrong. I do not think that anybody is born knowing everything. We do have geniuses in the world but some things in life are taught through experience. How would we know how to treat someone right when you have never been treated right? How would we know what love is if somebody didn't show us first? Children learn to speak and walk by observing others. Even babies learn to experience the world through their senses: smell, taste, sight, hearing, and touch.

As adults we experience the world around us through our senses also. If we learned through our senses and through imitation as a child, then it is only natural that we learn through our senses and through observation as an adult. We use senses, imitation, and observation in our relationships to interpret how we feel when we are with another person. Our feelings and emotions are deeper toward a person based on the amount of time spent with them using our senses. When we are in relationships, we imitate what we have learned and observed by storing these details in our hearts, memories, and mind. That is why you can still miss a person years after you have separated.

What happens when we have been treated badly and we get into a new relationship? We reenact our experiences from our old relationship in our new one. In order to change our behavior, we have to change our thinking. We have to relearn the right way to show that we love or care for someone despite all the bad things we have learned from old relationships.

Being in a relationship takes work. We cannot be there for a person physically until we learn how to be there for a person on a mental level. Before a boxer goes into the ring with his opponent, he practices or prepares for battle first. I have never seen a fighter get into a ring without any prior preparation. It can be done but I can tell you that the results are not going to be pretty. What happens is that he is caught off guard; he may end up losing the fight because he was not physically or mentally prepared for the battle.

The same principle applies to getting into a relationship before you are ready. Even if he is a good man, you will not be properly prepared if you do not prepare your mind for this new relationship. It's like getting ready to pay the cashier and paying with trash and money at the same time. You reached in your pocket to pay but you also pulled out the trash in your pocket without meaning to. Well, relationships go the same way. Whatever is in you is going to come out. And it always comes out when you think that it was gone. So it is very important to go through the cleansing process of the mind. So when you get into a new relationship, you give just your heart and not the trash from your past relationships.

"HURT GRAVE"

Write a letter to the man or men that you are still hurting over. Be truthful about your feelings. Tell them what is bothering you about the past relationship. This is a letter that you do not have to actually send to them. All you have to do is express your feelings and get all the painful emotions out. You do not have to put your name in the letter if you do not want to. If you decide to put your name in the letter then that is also okay. You feel that you are ready to move on and this may be closure for you.

When you are finished writing the letter, find a secret place to bury it in the ground. The symbolism of this action is to bury the pain that you have felt in the past. You are giving closure to this hurtful feeling by acknowledging that this feeling must die in order for you to go on with life.

You can actually dress up in black to represent mourning or you can dress up in bright colors that represent a happy feeling from the new absence of this pain. The main purpose of the ceremony is to acknowledge you are moving on with life because these negative feelings are now gone.

EMBRACE YOUR STRENGTH

For women who are religious, remember that your religion plays an essential part in your life. Your source of strength is the strength that is in you. You do not have to endure this pain alone because God is always with you. He will help you cope with the pain. Ask for God's love to heal your heart. Ask that he gives you strength to forgive the men that have hurt you. You can recite scriptures when you are hurting. You can pray and express your feelings to God when you are feeling down. You may not feel like confiding in those around you but you can always tell God what is bothering you. He already knows. Get involved in prayer groups that pray for one another. There are still good men out there. Just believe that one day you will find him. And remember not to lose sight of your hope and vision.

EXERCISE THE BODY AND MIND

Many people like yoga because it allows them to stretch their body and relax their mind at the same time. Stretching helps relieve tight and tense muscles in the body. Yoga relieves stress because you have to clear your mind of worries in order to stretch your body. While you are relieving tension from the body, you are also relieving tension from the mind. Try to practice this technique for at least fifteen minutes every day. Consider using this technique twice a day whenever you feel more stressed and tired.

USE IMAGINATION TO BELIEVE

Sometimes we think that imagination is just for kids. As adults we often forget that imagination is what keeps hope alive in our hearts. There is nothing wrong with being positive and using your imagination to hope for the best. Sometimes we laugh at kids because their dreams seem too big for just a little person. Kids can teach us a thing or two when it comes to using imagination. Imagination helps us envision the best possible life for ourselves. Your thinking and your imagination are linked together. They are almost like identical twins. What you think in your mind has a tendency to come true in reality. Your thoughts have massive power that influences the kind of day that you are going to have. Your thoughts even have power to imagine what kind of person you're looking to be with. Every day, imagine the kind of person you would like to be with. Imagine living happily and stress-free with this person. After a bad relationship, we imagine all men are the same. We become too afraid to give our heart away. We imagine scenarios of being hurt by any new man that comes into our lives. Instead of giving power to negativity, give power to positive thoughts. Imagine scenario after scenario of being with a good man, one that is different from the previous men you have dated. You will be surprised how this will impact the kind of men you meet. Remember that there is nothing wrong with dreaming as long as you keep your dreams alive.

BREATHE OUT THE PAIN

Try to incorporate breathing exercises into your everyday routine. If you feel that you are becoming anxious, release this tension with long deep breaths. Release them very slowly. After you have released your anxiety, say a positive word that is peaceful. Breathe again and say another word that brings you peace. What you are doing is you are releasing negative energy and replacing it with a positive outlook on life. Once you have breathed all the negative energy out, sit down and drink a glass of lemonade or tea. Prop up your feet and just relax. Take time to enjoy the peace. Your mind and body will thank you for caring so much about them.

FORGIVE THE OFFENDER

It is important not to carry around hurtful feelings for too long. It is okay to feel hurt as long as you release it. There is nothing you can do to change what the person has done to you. I'm not saying that you should not realize that you have been hurt and go through a grieving process. What I am saying is a grieving process is exactly what it means. It is a process where you go through it and come out of it. Some women make the mistake of never finishing the process. They grieve for years and years without enjoying their life.

Try not to focus on just your feelings. Examine and come to grips with how you feel but also realize that hurting people will hurt others. Sometimes when people are hurting themselves, they come across to others as hurtful. Some men may have had a hard life that causes them to act the way they are acting. If that is the case, give them time to deal with their pain. Do not let someone else's bitterness enter your life. This person may not be at a point in their life that they can love anyone else. If someone is hurting you, let them go. You might have been a blessing just by saying an encouraging word to them.

No matter how much pain a person is feeling that does not give them the right to treat anyone poorly. Never make excuses for anyone but rationalize the situation in your mind so that you can go on. Some men do not know how to treat others because they have not been trained or showed affection themselves. Some men have allowed their hurt to conquer their heart. Therefore, these men treat women the way that they feel on the inside. Do not waste energy trying to get back at these men. Instead give them space and forgive them so that you can move on. Holding onto pain only makes your heart bitter. The bitterness squeezes all the love out of your heart, causing your heart to become empty and hollow. You can't let other people in because you have your guard up. You become like the men that hurt you without even realizing it. When people are hurting, they want to pass on pain instead of getting rid of it. Don't let a man pass on his pain and issues to you. Stop it from spreading by letting the pain go before someone else gets infected. Pain is a heart disease that spreads until you decide that it ends with you. Make a choice you will not spread pain; instead, choose to spread joy and hope.

If you are not careful, then you will hurt others unintentionally because you have all that pain in your heart. Pain is like gas. You cannot drive a car without gas. Well if you build up enough pain in your heart, if helps fuel your passion to take revenge. Sometimes good men are targeted and they get hurt. If they get hurt then they fill their heart up with gas and have the potential to hurt other women. The cycle continues until you just have a lot of hurting people in the world. Only when you release the pain do you find relief and peace in your heart.

What you can do for the men that have hurt you is say good things about them. This will probably be the hardest thing that you had to do in your life. Wish them well in life but move on. The person that is causing you pain is at a point in their life where they can only give you what is in their heart. If pain is all that they have to give then give them space and just wish them the best. Live your life so that you can encourage and love others. If it helps, you can go to a private place and let go of dreams and good things in the sky. Blow up a balloon and place little notes in them wishing the people that have hurt you well. Wish them healing and happiness to replace the pain they may be feeling. You can also write happy things that you would like to happen to you in the notes. Let them fly away in the wind of dreams. Eventually these balloons will pop, but it never hurts to have a dream or two lying here or there. You do not have to put your name on the notes. The goal is to release your dreams into the sky so that they touch others. One day you may see these dreams return back to you in hope.

WHAT MEDITATION CAN BRING

Meditation focuses on good things and prevents negative things from entering the mind. It is an avenue for attaining peace that many people strive to obtain every day from their busy schedules. Meditation is simply enjoying the quietness of your own mind. You do not have to sit on the floor with your legs crossed to meditate. You can be sitting down, standing up, walking, or running. It can happen anywhere at any time. It can even happen in a noisy setting. Yes, meditation is simply focusing on something good and centering your whole attention on this good thing for hours. When you finish meditating, you will feel like you just took a three-week vacation for free.

Have you ever been so focused on what you were thinking about that you didn't hear the person talking to you or you didn't see the person walk toward you? What happened is you were so focused on what you were thinking about that your mind blocked everything out. That's the power of meditation! You can take it anywhere and all it requires is focus and a clear mind.

Try meditating on good things for at least fifteen minutes a day. Every day, take some "me time" that allows you to focus on yourself, your feelings, and happy thoughts. You can't go wrong.

RUNNING OR WALKING

For at least thirty minutes a day, try walking or running. This keeps your self-esteem high and creates a healthy lifestyle.. You can create an everyday routine that allows you to walk or run to get rid of stress. You feel good while doing it, so why not keep up what makes you feel good? Instead of being tempted to eat, this routine will give your mind a way of releasing stress without feeling a need to overeat.

DO WHAT YOU LOVE

Spend time everyday doing something that you love. It can be drawing, sewing, music, singing, or another talent that you do well. Do not focus on the man that you don't have in your life right now. Focus on the gift that you have inside of you. Use your energy to focus on what is good in your life. Focus your attention on this positive aspect of who you are.

Do not focus on what you cannot do. A lot of times when we are not in a relationship or have just broken up with someone, low-self esteem sinks in. We wonder why no men are looking at us. Are we worthy to be loved? Should we just accept anyone that wants to be with us? With these questions in mind, we start to feel bad about who we are. You don't have to feel this way because a man is not in your life right now. You can feel good about who you are and what gifts you have to share with the world. Look at it like this: not being in a relationship right now helps you get to know yourself more. Then when you are with someone, you have much more of yourself to share with them. They get you and what your soul has to offer them.

FEEL WARMED UP?

These are just a few techniques to get you started. Find creative ways that help you release your pain or the stressful feelings that you feel on an everyday basis. There will be days when you will feel as if you are losing your mind, that the world is crashing on you and you are flooded with emotions that you don't understand. It is important that each woman discovers her own emotional support system. That way, if a man is not in your life, you won't feel a great dependence on him to help you find balance in dealing with your emotions. Any of the exercises I mentioned above can help relieve stress for women and even men. Find your own way that works well for you. Remember to take time out for yourself each day. Find a way to balance your time to keep stress at a low level in your life.

CONCLUSION

I hope you have enjoyed the book. I appreciate you so much for the kind of woman that you are. Always remember to love yourself and be happy in life. There is so much in life that you can do and you owe it to yourself to show the world your ability. Waiting on the right man to share your life with is difficult but it is not impossible. You are worth more than settling for a man because the right one has not come yet. Every woman is unique and has her own inner beauty. It's up to you to find and mold that beauty and make it into your own. No one else can mold the beauty that is inside of you but you. Never ever let any man take your shine away from you and tell you that you are not worth anything because you are.

The right man will come along but you cannot lose hope and you can't rush patience. I do believe that everyone has a soul mate. And there is a particular time that their paths will cross and they are going to meet each other. The challenge is in not giving up before your paths have a chance to cross. Some men will come into your life and try to make it seem like they are the ones that you are supposed to be with. But if you don't feel like this man is the right one or you feel doubtful about him then do not ignore that feeling. When the right one comes along, you will know and he will not send your mind on rollercoaster rides trying to figure out ways to make the relationship work.

I'm not telling you anything that I have not experienced or seen from other women's relationships. I wanted to write this book to help women and give them hope that a good man is out there, that they should just wait and stop inviting the wrong men into their life over and over. Love still exists. Good relationships still exist. Chances are if you have picked up this book and read it all the way through then that means that you are tired of the relationships that you have experienced in the past. If that is the case then you're on your way to experiencing relationships differently in the future. I wish you nothing but the best. And I want you to remember that when a man really cares for you, he will treat you with love, care, and respect. But if any man ever tries to tell you different, "Run girl run!"